Let's Cook!

Let's Cook!

55 Quick and Easy Recipes for People with Intellectual Disability

Elizabeth D. Riesz, PhD
Anne Kissack, MPH, RD

THE EXPERIMENT

NEW YORK

The Experiment, LLC
220 East 23rd Street, Suite 600
New York, NY 10010-4658
theexperimentpublishing.com

Library of Congress Cataloging-in-Publication Data

Names: Riesz, Elizabeth Dunkman, author. | Kissack, Anne, author.
Title: Let's cook! : 55 quick and easy recipes for people with intellectual
  disability / Elizabeth D. Riesz, PhD; Anne Kissack, MPH, RD.
Description: 3rd [edition]. | New York : The Experiment, [2021] | Includes
  index.
Identifiers: LCCN 2021000265 (print) | LCCN 2021000266 (ebook) | ISBN
  9781615197668 (spiral bound) | ISBN 9781615197675 (ebook)
Subjects: LCSH: Cooking for people with mental disabilities. | Cooking,
  American. | Quick and easy cooking. | LCGFT: Cookbooks.
Classification: LCC TX652 .R537 2021 (print) | LCC TX652 (ebook) | DDC
  641.5087--dc23
LC record available at https://lccn.loc.gov/2021000265
LC ebook record available at https://lccn.loc.gov/2021000266

ISBN 978-1-61519-766-8
Ebook ISBN 978-1-61519-767-5

Cover and text design by Beth Bugler, Sarah Bennet, Douglas Allan, and Lime Valley Advertising
Cover photographs by Appletree Press, Inc.

Manufactured in China

First printing May 2021
10 9 8 7 6 5 4 3 2 1

DEDICATION

Deep appreciation and gratitude to —

Our daughter, Sarah Kathleen, born with Down syndrome: She finally walked at three and a half years, and now inspires us as she holds two community jobs, participates in Special Olympics swimming and skiing, sings in a special choir, belongs to a fitness club, cooks nourishing meals, and maintains her healthy lifestyle.

My parents, Cornelia E. and William E. Dunkman (both deceased): They overcame the shock of their first grandchild's condition, loved her, and celebrated each new milestone. My mother, an award-winning cook, introduced me to the pleasure of cooking.

Peg Lawrenson, Sarah's last high school teacher: Committed to her students' successful transition to adult living, she guided their growth in vocational, community (library, bus, fitness center), communication, and cooking skills. Peg developed Sarah's user-friendly recipe format and assembled class recipes in a binder for each student at graduation.

F. J. Puga, MD, cardiac surgeon at the Mayo Clinic (Rochester, MN): When Sarah was twelve, his skill in repairing her heart defects resulted in her increased growth, strength, and endurance.

Sarah's supported living house staff and their administrators at Reach for Your Potential, Inc.: They assist Sarah to make healthy food choices and to maintain her exercise routine.

Most especially to my husband, Peter: At the beginning, he assisted with six months of round-the-clock feeding. With his companionship, Sarah has become a star Frisbee player. He is her favorite bowling partner and Monopoly competitor. For more than three decades, he has supported me in activities related to Sarah's growth and education.

— Elizabeth D. Riesz, PhD
2016

Heartfelt thanks and gratitude to —

My parents, James and Susan Sypniewski, for the many loving sacrifices they made to provide an education and support experiences that have afforded me the many blessings of my life.

My husband, Phil, and children, Theresa and Anthony, who have shown me unconditional support and love.

— Anne Kissack, MPH, RD
2016

THE STORY BEHIND *LET'S COOK!*

This cookbook is based on the recipes developed over time by and for my daughter, Sarah, who was born with Down syndrome. It is important that Sarah have healthy foods because in addition to Down syndrome, she had three problems with her heart that caused her to grow very slowly and left her physically weak. With corrective surgeries, exercise, and a healthy diet, she grew strong and healthy.

Sarah started making lunch and dinner foods as a teenager. Her teachers joined me in helping find recipes. Sarah cooked at school and at home with a life skills coach. Her father and I loved coming home from work on Mondays! That's the day of the week that Sarah cooked a main dish, vegetable, and salad for our family.

Her coach helped her follow recipes and showed her how to stay safe in the kitchen. Eventually, Sarah cooked twice a week at home, and over the years, her recipe collection expanded. Her recipe collection became the foundation for this cookbook. Today, Sarah cooks meals in her supported living residence, taking turns with housemates. She is often asked for her recipes by friends, teachers, and service providers, and praised for the tasty meals she prepares.

Coauthor Anne began creatively working with the recipes as part of her Master in Public Health practicum. She standardized recipes, contributed new recipes to balance the food groups, developed additional nutrition notes, and added food and kitchen safety standards. Anne went on to emphasize meal-planning strategies and developed the graphic content for categorizing recipes into food groups and balanced meals.

Anne's work laid the groundwork for a publishable cookbook. This cookbook, we believe, will help you to create recipes that you will enjoy, to plan meals using many food groups, to select healthy snacks, and to eat well in restaurants.

As we say at the close of each successful recipe, may you . . . serve and ENJOY!

—*Elizabeth (Betsy) D. Riesz, PhD, coauthor*
December 2009

WELCOME TO
Let's Cook!

As you read the story behind *Let's Cook!*, it becomes clear that this book is the result of many voices—individuals who care about the health and safety of those who are challenged to prepare their own meals. Project staff listened as focus group participants talked about what they needed to make healthy meals on their own.

Yes, they needed to know what to cook as well as how to cook. But, they also asked for a cookbook to be designed and written just for them with specific qualities—recipes in large print, with lots of food pictures, with clear preparation steps—and above all, they wanted a cookbook that couldn't be misinterpreted as a children's cookbook.

We've worked tirelessly to meet those challenges. We can assure you the recipes work. Recipes were triple taste tested and prepared by a number of individuals (at various ability levels) who love to cook. The easy-to-make recipes are in large print, written at a third grade or lower reading level, and the step-by-step preparations take the guesswork out of what to do. The finished recipe is photographed alone and again, as part of a healthy, balanced meal in the appropriate serving size.

We know you'll treasure your personal copy of *Let's Cook!* We hope you take great pleasure in preparing wonderful food from *Let's Cook!* and that the recipes help you take action for a longer, stronger, and happier life.

—*Linda Hachfeld, MPH, RD, editor*
December 2009

Contents

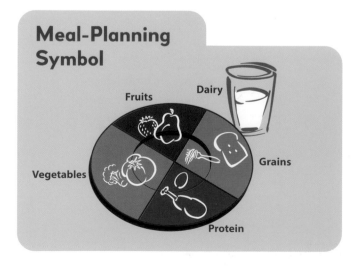

Meal-Planning Symbol

Fruits · Dairy · Grains · Protein · Vegetables

Cornerstone of Good Health

Build a Healthy Eating Style

Everyone has their own eating style. I can build a healthy eating style that fits me. ChooseMyPlate.gov reminds me to:

- **Eat a variety of foods in the right amount from each food group.**
- **Focus on making healthy food and beverage choices from all five food groups.**

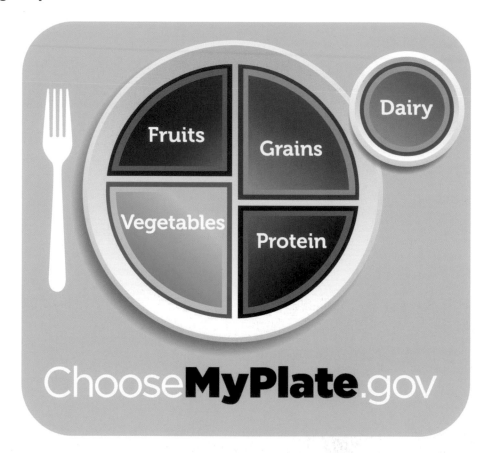

Everything I eat and drink matters. Most foods fit into five food groups. Each food group has a color. The colors—**orange purple green red blue**—stand for the five food groups.

When I eat foods from each food group every day and limit added fats, refined grains, sugar, and salt, I have a healthy diet.

When I make wise food choices and have physical activity (like walking or sports) every day, my lifestyle is healthy.

How Much to Eat

Each person is different. The amount of food I need to eat is based on my age, gender, and level of physical activity. This chart shows me how much to eat as a serving and how much to eat every day from each food group.

MyPlate food groups	Count as 1 serving		Total servings every day
GRAINS *Make at least half my grains whole*	1 slice of bread or ½ a bun 1 cup ready-to-eat cereal ½ cup cooked cereal ½ cup cooked rice or pasta	1 (6-inch) corn or flour tortilla 2 (5-inch) taco shells 3 cups air-popped popcorn 6 saltine-type crackers	3 to 5 servings (3- to 5-ounce equivalents)
VEGETABLES *Vary my veggies*	1 cup raw vegetables ½ cup cooked vegetables 6 baby carrots 1 medium boiled or baked potato		2 to 3 servings (2½ to 3 cups)
FRUITS *Focus on whole fruits*	1 small piece fresh fruit ½ cup canned fruit (in own juice) ½ cup 100% fruit juice 2 Tablespoons dried fruit (like raisins)		1½ to 2 servings (1½ to 2 cups)
DAIRY *Eat calcium-rich foods*	1 cup low-fat milk or calcium-fortified alternative milk 1 (6-ounce) container low-fat yogurt 1½ ounces hard cheese	½ cup cottage cheese **Other Non-Dairy Sources of Calcium:** 1 cup spinach 3 ounces canned sardines	2 to 3 servings (2 to 3 cups)
PROTEIN *Go lean with protein*	1 egg 2 Tablespoons nut butter (like peanut) ½ cup cooked beans, lentils, or split peas 1 small (3-ounce) chicken breast 1 small (2 to 3 ounces) lean ground beef	3 to 4 ounces fresh fish ¼ cup canned tuna (½ of a 5-ounce can) 1 (3-ounce) soy or bean burger patty ½ cup tofu ⅓ cup hummus	2 to 3 servings (5- to 6½-ounce equivalents)

Please go to choosemyplate.gov/resources/MyPlatePlan to find out what and how much to eat for my age, gender, height, weight, and level of physical activity.

Healthy Serving Sizes

The amount of food I eat is a serving. A healthy serving of food can be measured with a measuring cup or spoon. Or I can use parts of my hand to guide me.

Use a measuring cup or my fist to measure:

- Casseroles
- Cereal (ready-to-eat)
- Fresh fruit
- Milk
- Salad
- Soup

My palm = 3 ounces of meat
Use my palm to measure:

- Beef
- Chicken breast
- Fish (like salmon)
- Pork (like a pork chop)

Each glass holds 1 cup of milk. Measure 1 cup of milk into my favorite glass. Now I know how high to pour milk in my glass for a healthy serving.

Use a Tablespoon measure or my thumb to measure:

- Cream cheese
- Mayonnaise
- Oil
- Peanut butter
- Salad dressing
- Sour cream

 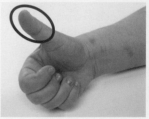

Use a half-cup measure or my cupped hand to measure:

- Brown rice
- Cooked cereal
- Cottage cheese
- Cooked vegetables
- Mashed potatoes
- Pasta (like spaghetti)

Use a teaspoon measure or the tip of my thumb to measure:

- Jam and jelly
- Soft-tub margarine

Build a Healthy Meal

Use MyPlate

MyPlate shows me which foods I can use to build a healthy meal.

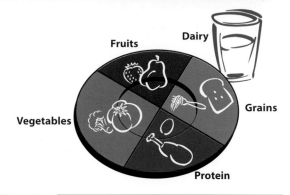

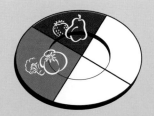

Half of my plate should be fruits and vegetables.

The other half of my plate should be grains and protein.

I need 3 dairy servings a day. I can drink low-fat milk, soy milk, or Lactaid with my meals. Or, I can eat low-fat cheese or yogurt.

MyPlate Healthy Meals

Foods from three, four, or five food groups make a healthy meal. Here are samples of three healthy meals.

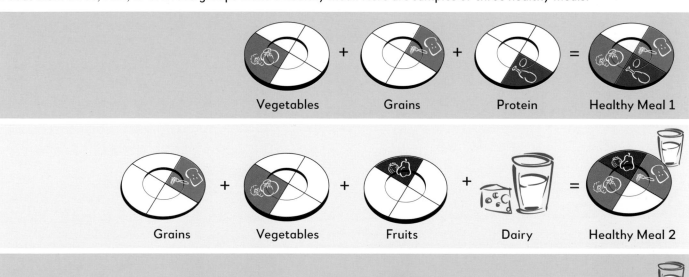

Vegetables + Grains + Protein = Healthy Meal 1

Grains + Vegetables + Fruits + Dairy = Healthy Meal 2

Protein + Grains + Vegetables + Fruits + Dairy = Healthy Meal 3

Plan a Healthy Meal

The recipes in *Let's Cook!* are organized by MyPlate food groups. Some recipes use ingredients from more than one food group and can belong to two or three food groups.

Let's Cook! **Recipe Guide**

MyPlate Food Group
Each recipe is color-coded in the same color as the MyPlate food group it best fits.

Number of Servings
Each recipe tells me the number of servings in the recipe and how much to eat as a serving.

Meal Planning
The MyPlate and the ChooseMyPlate icons show the food groups in this recipe and on my plate. The dairy glass shows the recipe has a dairy serving.

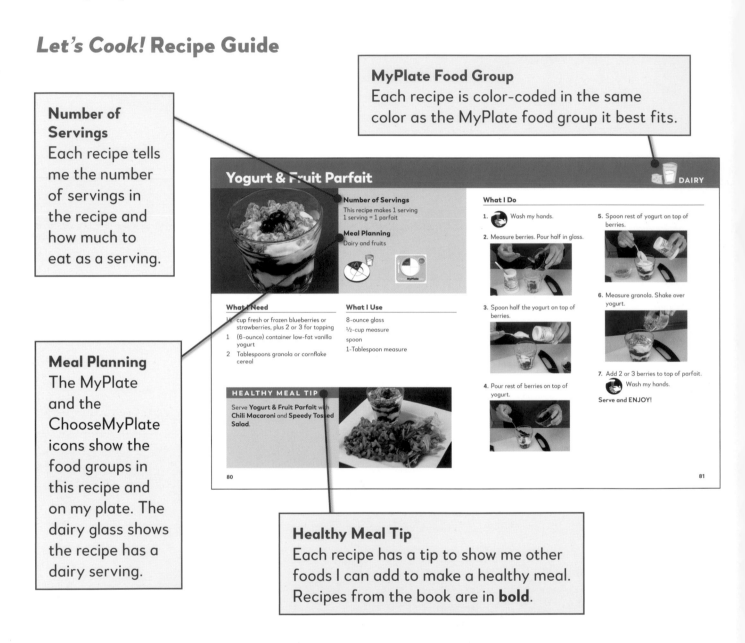

Yogurt & Fruit Parfait — DAIRY

Number of Servings
This recipe makes 1 serving
1 serving = 1 parfait

Meal Planning
Dairy and fruits

What I Need
1/2 cup fresh or frozen blueberries or strawberries, plus 2 or 3 for topping
1 (6-ounce) container low-fat vanilla yogurt
2 Tablespoons granola or cornflake cereal

What I Use
8-ounce glass
1/2-cup measure
spoon
1-Tablespoon measure

HEALTHY MEAL TIP
Serve **Yogurt & Fruit Parfait** with **Chili Macaroni** and **Speedy Tossed Salad**.

What I Do
1. Wash my hands.
2. Measure berries. Pour half in glass.
3. Spoon half the yogurt on top of berries.
4. Pour rest of berries on top of yogurt.
5. Spoon rest of yogurt on top of berries.
6. Measure granola. Shake over yogurt.
7. Add 2 or 3 berries to top of parfait.
   Wash my hands.
   Serve and ENJOY!

80

81

Healthy Meal Tip
Each recipe has a tip to show me other foods I can add to make a healthy meal. Recipes from the book are in **bold**.

For nutrition information about the recipes, see pages 130–31. Nutrition information includes calories and values for protein, carbohydrates, fat, saturated fat, sodium, and fiber per serving. In addition, carbohydrate choices and diabetic exchanges are provided.

Let's Cook! recipes are colorful and fun. They are tasty and healthy. We hope you'll enjoy them as much as we do.

Samples of Healthy Meals

Let's Cook! is filled with recipes that can make several healthy meals. Be sure to look for the Healthy Meal Tip with each recipe. Here are more healthy meals using the recipes from *Let's Cook!*

Start with **Tater Tot Casserole**. Add a green leafy salad and finish with a **Baked Apple**.

Start with **Meat Loaf**. Add a **Baked Potato** and **Golden Glazed Carrots**.

Start with **Pork Chop Apple Bake**. Add your favorite **Microwave Vegetables** and finish with **Florida Citrus Salad**.

Start with a **Turkey Burger**. Add **Confetti Corn** and finish with **Apple Grape Salad**. Enjoy a small glass of milk as a beverage.

More Samples of Healthy Meals

Start with a bowl of **Chili**. Add whole grain crackers and a garden salad. Finish with the **Yogurt & Fruit Parfait**.

Start with **Apricot Curry Chicken**. Add **Rice Vegetable Medley** and finish with tapioca pudding with a cherry on top!

Start with **Turkey Rice Casserole**. Add **Golden Glazed Carrots** and finish with **Florida Citrus Salad**.

More Healthy Meals

- Serve the **Fish Sandwich** with **Microwave Frozen Vegetables** and a fresh fruit cup.

- Serve **Meat Loaf** with **Confetti Corn** and **Pineapple Cabbage Salad**.

- Serve **Baked Salmon** with a **Baked Potato** and **Apple Slaw**.

- Serve **Veggie Omelet** with a toasted English muffin and fresh grapes.

- Serve **Western Skillet** with a green leafy salad and a fresh fruit cup.

- Serve **Baked Chicken** with **Microwave Frozen Vegetables** and **Pineapple Carrot Salad**.

Food and Kitchen Safety

Hand Washing Tips

Stay healthy by cooking safely. Germs that I can't see can make me sick. The most important rule to follow when I cook is "wash my hands" often.

To be safe, I will wash my hands:

✓ Before I cook

✓ After I cough or sneeze

✓ After I touch raw meat

✓ When I have a cut or sore

✓ After I go to the bathroom

✓ Before I eat

I need to use soap and warm water for at least 20 seconds (the time it takes to sing the birthday song) to kill germs.

Recipe Symbol

"Wash my hands"

Kitchen Safety Tips

1. Keep my cooking tools clean. Wash all bowls, spoons, plates, knives, and cutting boards in the dishwasher or by hand in the sink when I'm done using them. Let the dishes air dry when done washing.

2. Use soap, hot water, and a dishcloth to wash kitchen counters and the stovetop every time I use the kitchen.

3. Throw meat wrappers away immediately. Take out the trash often.

4. Wipe all meat juices off kitchen counters with a paper towel. Throw the paper towel away. Use a dishcloth with soap and hot water to wipe the counter clean. Wash hands again after cleaning.

More Food and Kitchen Safety

Food Safety Tips

1. Wash all fruits and vegetables before I use them.

2. Use one cutting board and sharp knife for raw meat. Use a different cutting board and sharp knife for other foods.

3. If I have only 1 cutting board, I will make sure to cut all vegetables for the recipe first. Then I will cut the meat. I will remember to always wash my cutting board and knife after every time I use them.

4. Use a timer to cook foods completely.

5. Cook and stir raw meat until all the meat is brown. Use a food thermometer to test when the meat is cooked completely.

Visit *foodsafety.gov/food-safety-charts/meat-poultry-charts* for food safety tips or call USDA Meat and Poultry Hotline at (888) 674-6854

Cooking Temperatures for Meat	
Chicken, turkey	165°F
Egg dishes	160°F
Fish	145°F
Ground beef, pork	160°F
Leftovers	165°F
Roasts and chops	145–160°F

Recipe Symbol

 Look for this symbol in the recipes when a timer is needed.

Safety Rules for Leftovers

1. Follow the 2-Hour Rule. Never allow food to sit at temperatures between 40°F and 140°F for more than 2 hours.

2. Always cover leftovers to keep bacteria out. Wrap leftovers (like turkey burgers) with wax paper or plastic wrap. Then put into a storage container. Now I can take out what I need and leave the rest in the freezer.

3. Place leftovers (like salads and casseroles) in a storage container with a lid that seals.

4. Use a label and permanent marker to write the name of the food and date it was made. Place the label on the outside of the container.

5. Place containers in the fridge or freezer right away.

6. Leftovers can be kept in the fridge for 3 to 4 days or frozen for 3 to 4 months.

7. Remember to keep cold foods cold when using leftovers for a bag lunch.

8. Use a food thermometer to cook leftovers to a safe temperature (see page 12).

What I Use: Kitchen Tools

Here are the tools (equipment and utensils) that I will use to make the recipes in *Let's Cook!* I don't need a lot of stuff. Each recipe tells me what tools to use under the heading **What I Use**.

Pots
(small, medium, and large with lid)
Use on the stovetop.

Skillets
(small, medium, and deep with lid)
Use on the stovetop.

Baking dishes (glass)
These are microwave-safe and oven-proof.

Loaf pan (metal or glass)
Both can be used in the oven. Only the glass loaf pan can be used in the microwave.

Pie plate (glass)
Microwave-safe and oven-proof

Cookie sheet (metal)
Use only in the oven.

Strainer

 When you see this symbol place the strainer in the sink.

Can opener

Wash can opener after each use.

Vegetable peeler

Most vegetables just need scrubbing. Don't peel unless the recipe says so.

Glass bowls

(small, medium, and large)
Use for mixing; also microwave-safe.

Cutting board and sharp knife

Use one for raw meats. Use another for cutting all other foods.

Measuring cups (glass)

Use these to measure liquids like milk or water.

Measuring cups (metal or plastic)

Use these to measure dry ingredients like shredded cheese.

Measuring spoons

1-Tablespoon, 1-teaspoon, ½- and ¼-teaspoon measures

More Kitchen Tools

Wooden spoon
Use for mixing and stirring.

Whisk
Use to beat eggs to make bubbles on top.

Spatula (or rubber spatula)
Use for mixing and scraping food out of cans.

Turner (or pancake turner)
Use to flip burgers, omelets, and lift food from the pan to the plate.

Oven mitt and pot holder
Use these to remove hot food from the oven, stovetop, or microwave.

Food thermometer
Use to check that raw meat is fully cooked. Please see the Cooking Temperatures for Meat chart on page 12.

Timer
Set the timer to the amount of time to cook food completely.

 Look for this symbol in the recipes when I use a timer.

Recipe Symbols

 Preheat oven. Turn oven to temperature in recipe.

 Place strainer in sink.

 Use timer.

ChooseMyPlate.gov

Let's Cook! Shopping List

To download and print more shopping lists,
go to bit.ly/expletscook.

Recipes I Plan to Make:

_____

_____

_____

✔ **Check to see I have these foods:**	**Foods I need to buy today:**
GRAINS ❏ instant brown rice ❏ whole grain cereal ❏ whole grain pasta ❏ whole wheat bread ❏ _____	_____ _____ _____ _____ _____
VEGETABLES ❏ frozen vegetables ❏ leafy greens ❏ onions ❏ tomatoes ❏ _____	_____ _____ _____ _____ _____
FRUITS ❏ apples ❏ bananas ❏ oranges ❏ raisins ❏ _____	_____ _____ _____ _____ _____
DAIRY ❏ low-fat milk ❏ low-fat yogurt ❏ reduced-fat cheese ❏ string cheese ❏ _____	_____ _____ _____ _____ _____
PROTEIN ❏ canned tuna in water ❏ chicken breasts ❏ eggs ❏ lean ground turkey or extra lean ground beef ❏ _____	_____ _____ _____ _____ _____
OTHER ❏ canned low-sodium soup ❏ low-sugar jam/jelly ❏ olive oil ❏ soft-tub margarine ❏ _____	_____ _____ _____ _____ _____

Indian Rice

Number of Servings

This recipe makes 4 servings
1 serving = ¾ cup

Meal Planning

Grains and vegetables

What I Need

1	cup instant brown rice (dry)
1	cup plus 2 Tablespoons water

Nonstick cooking spray

⅓	cup frozen or fresh chopped onion
1	cup frozen mixed vegetables
⅓	cup raisins
¼	teaspoon garlic powder
¼	teaspoon ground ginger
¼	teaspoon ground cinnamon
¼	teaspoon ground cumin

Dash of black pepper

What I Use

medium microwave-safe glass bowl

medium pot

1-cup measure

⅓-cup measure

wooden spoon

spatula and fork

measuring spoons

clear plastic wrap

timer

cutting board (for fresh onion)

sharp knife (for fresh onion)

HEALTHY MEAL TIP

Serve **Indian Rice** with **Baked Salmon** and **Spinach Apple Salad**.

What I Do

1. Wash my hands.

2. Measure rice. Pour in bowl.

3. Measure 1 cup water. Add to rice. Cover bowl tightly with plastic wrap.

4. Microwave on HIGH POWER for 4 minutes. Let rice sit for 5 minutes. Carefully remove plastic wrap. Fluff rice with fork. Set aside.

5. Spray pot with cooking spray. Measure and add 2 Tablespoons water. Place pot on stove.

6. If using fresh onion: On cutting board, chop into tiny pieces with sharp knife. Measure onion and pour into pot. Cook on MEDIUM heat for 2 minutes.

7. Measure frozen vegetables. Pour into pot.

8. Measure and stir into pot—
   - raisins
   - ginger
   - cumin
   - garlic powder
   - cinnamon
   - pepper

9. Add cooked rice to pot. Stir with wooden spoon.

10. Cover pot with lid and cook for 5 minutes on MEDIUM heat. Use timer. Turn off stove.

Serve and ENJOY!

Instant Brown Rice

Number of Servings

This recipe makes 3 servings
1 serving = ½ cup

Meal Planning

Grains

What I Need

1   cup instant brown rice (dry)
1   cup water

What I Use

small microwave-safe glass bowl OR small pot with lid

1-cup measure

metal fork

wooden spoon (for stovetop)

clear plastic wrap (for microwave)

timer

oven mitt and pot holder (for microwave)

HEALTHY MEAL TIP

Serve **Instant Brown Rice** with **Chicken Stir-Fry** and sugar-free gelatin with fruit.

What I Do

Microwave Directions

1. Wash my hands.

2. Measure rice. Pour into microwave-safe bowl.

3. Measure water. Add to rice.

4. Cover bowl tightly with plastic wrap.

Microwave for 4 minutes on HIGH POWER.

5. Let rice sit for 5 minutes. Carefully remove bowl from microwave. Use oven mitt and pot holder.

6. Carefully remove plastic wrap. Stir rice with fork.

Serve and ENJOY!

Stovetop Directions

1. Wash my hands.

2. Measure water in small pot. Place pot on stove. Heat on HIGH. Water will be boiling.

3. Measure rice. Add rice to pot. Stir. Let water return to boiling.

4. Reduce heat to LOW; cover and simmer 5 minutes.

 Use timer.

5. Remove pot from heat. Turn off stove. Stir rice with wooden spoon. Cover.

6. Let rice sit for 5 minutes or until water is gone. Stir with fork.

Serve and ENJOY!

Rice Vegetable Medley

Number of Servings

This recipe makes 6 servings
1 serving = ¾ cup

Meal Planning

Grains and vegetables

What I Need

1   medium zucchini

1   (10-ounce) can reduced-sodium chicken broth

²/₃   cup water

1   teaspoon dried dill weed

2   cups instant brown rice (dry)

1   medium tomato

¼   cup Parmesan cheese

What I Use

large pot with lid

cutting board and sharp knife

can opener

1-cup measure

⅓-cup and ¼-cup measures

wooden spoon

1-teaspoon measure

timer

HEALTHY MEAL TIP

Serve **Rice Vegetable Medley** with **Apricot Curry Chicken** and tapioca pudding with a cherry on top.

What I Do

1. Wash my hands.

2. Rinse zucchini under cold running water.

3. On cutting board, use sharp knife to cut zucchini into small pieces. Put zucchini pieces in pot.

4. Open broth. Pour broth into pot.

5. Measure and add to pot—
   • water   • dill weed

6. Place pot on stove. Turn stove to HIGH.

    When broth starts to boil, set timer for 2 minutes.

7. Turn off stove when timer goes off. Remove pot from heat.

8. Add instant brown rice to pot. Cover with lid.

    Set timer for 5 minutes.

9. Rinse tomato under cold running water. On cutting board, use sharp knife to cut tomato into medium-size pieces.

10. When timer goes off, add tomato pieces to rice in pot.

11. Add Parmesan to rice. Stir gently with wooden spoon until well mixed.

Serve and ENJOY!

Saucepan Spaghetti

Number of Servings

This recipe makes 5 servings
1 serving = 1½ cups

Meal Planning

Grains, vegetables, dairy, and protein

What I Need

1   pound lean ground beef

1   (15-ounce) can low-sodium tomato sauce

1   Tablespoon dried onion

1   Tablespoon dried oregano

1   Tablespoon Worcestershire sauce

1   teaspoon sugar

½   teaspoon dried basil

¼   teaspoon black pepper

3½ cups water

1   (6-ounce) package whole wheat spaghetti noodles (dry)

1   cup shredded mozzarella/cheddar cheese

What I Use

serving plates

large skillet with lid

can opener

1-cup measure

½-cup measure

wooden spoon

measuring spoons

timer

oven mitts

HEALTHY MEAL TIP

Serve **Saucepan Spaghetti** with a fresh tossed salad and fresh fruit.

What I Do

1. Wash my hands.

2. Unwrap beef. Put beef in skillet. Throw away meat wrapper.
   Wash my hands.
   Clean counter (see page 11).

3. Place skillet on stove. Turn burner to MEDIUM heat. Use wooden spoon to break up beef.

4. Cook and stir beef until all the meat is brown.

5. Measure and add to skillet—
   - tomato sauce
   - sugar
   - dried onion
   - basil
   - oregano
   - pepper
   - Worcestershire sauce

6. Stir well with wooden spoon.

7. Measure water. Add water to skillet.

8. Open spaghetti package. Break spaghetti into pieces. Add spaghetti pieces to skillet.

9. Turn heat to HIGH. When water boils, turn to LOW. Cover skillet with lid.
    Set timer for 30 minutes. Cook. Stir now and then.

10. Use oven mitts to carefully remove skillet from stove. Ask for help if it's too heavy. Turn off stove.
     Wash my hands.

11. Place on plates with shredded cheese on top of each serving.

Serve and ENJOY!

Spaghetti for Four

Number of Servings

This recipe makes 4 servings
1 serving = ½ cup

Meal Planning

Grains

What I Need

8   cups water

8   ounces whole wheat spaghetti noodles (dry; ½ of 16-ounce box)

1   Tablespoon olive or canola oil

4   Tablespoons Parmesan cheese

Parsley (optional)

What I Use

4 serving plates

large 4-quart pot and strainer

medium bowl

1-cup measure

wooden spoon

1-Tablespoon measure

timer

oven mitts

HEALTHY MEAL TIP

Serve **Spaghetti** with **Meatballs** and garlic toast with **Pineapple Cabbage Salad**.

What I Do

1. Wash my hands.

   Place strainer in sink.

2. Measure water. Pour water into pot. Place pot on stove. Turn stove to HIGH heat. Boil water.

3. Measure dry spaghetti. Break spaghetti into pieces and put in medium bowl.

4. When water boils, carefully put spaghetti pieces in pot. Turn to MEDIUM heat.

5. When water boils again, stir spaghetti with wooden spoon.

6. Set timer for 8 minutes. Stir once again.

7. When timer rings, turn off heat.

8. With help, use oven mitt and carry pot to sink. Pour water and spaghetti into strainer. Drain well.

9. Pour spaghetti back into pot.

10. Add oil. Mix well.

11. To serve, place spaghetti on each plate.

12. Measure 1 Tablespoon Parmesan. Shake on each serving. Add parsley to each plate, if desired.

Serve and ENJOY!

Spanish Rice

Number of Servings

This recipe makes 3 servings
1 serving = ¾ cup

Meal Planning

Grains and protein

What I Need

1   recipe Instant Brown Rice, prepared (page 20)

5   vegetarian sausage links (from package)

½   cup spaghetti sauce

½   teaspoon dried oregano

¼   teaspoon dried basil

Parsley (optional)

What I Use

medium skillet

cutting board

sharp knife

wooden spoon

spatula

fork

measuring spoons

HEALTHY MEAL TIP

Serve **Spanish Rice** with **Cottage Cheese Tomato Salad**. Add fresh fruit.

What I Do

1. Wash my hands.

For Links

2. Remove sausage links from package. Put in skillet. Place skillet on stove. Turn stove to MEDIUM heat. Use fork to turn the links until they are brown and fully cooked, 12 to 13 minutes.

3. Turn off heat. Use fork to put links on cutting board.

4. On cutting board, use sharp knife to cut each link into 4 or 5 pieces. Put link pieces back in skillet.

 Wash my hands.

For Sauce

5. Measure spaghetti sauce. Pour into skillet.

6. Measure oregano and basil. Add to skillet.

7. Turn stove to MEDIUM. Stir until sauce bubbles.

8. Carefully add cooked brown rice to skillet. Stir well.

9. Turn off stove. Add parsley, if desired.

Serve and ENJOY!

Tortilla Sandwich Wrap

Number of Servings

This recipe makes 1 tortilla wrap
1 serving = 1 tortilla wrap

Meal Planning

Grains, vegetables, dairy, and protein

What I Need

2   lettuce leaves

1   (10-inch) whole wheat tortilla

1   Tablespoon fat-free, vegetable-flavored, soft cream cheese

2   slices (½ ounce each) sodium-reduced turkey breast

2   slices (½ ounce each) low-fat Swiss cheese

½   tomato (2 or 3 tomato slices)

What I Use

large plate

cutting board

sharp knife

table knife

1-Tablespoon measure

2 toothpicks

paper towel

HEALTHY MEAL TIP

Serve **Tortilla Sandwich Wrap** with **Corn Chowder** and fresh fruit.

What I Do

1. Wash my hands.

2. Wash lettuce leaves under cold running water. Wrap lettuce in paper towel to dry.

3. Place tortilla on large plate.

4. Measure 1 Tablespoon cream cheese.

5. With table knife, spread cream cheese on tortilla.

6. Place 2 slices turkey on tortilla.

7. Place 2 slices cheese on top of turkey.

8. Unwrap the lettuce. Put lettuce on top of cheese.

9. On cutting board, cut tomato in slices with sharp knife. Place 2 or 3 tomato slices on top of lettuce.

10. Roll tortilla into a tube shape.

11. Place toothpicks into wrap to help hold its shape. Cut in half.

 Wash my hands.

Serve and ENJOY!

Golden Glazed Carrots

Number of Servings

This recipe makes 3 servings
1 serving = ½ cup

Meal Planning

Vegetables

What I Need

1   Tablespoon olive oil

1½ cups baby carrots (prepackaged)

¼   cup water

2   Tablespoons brown sugar

Dash of salt-free seasoning, such as
Mrs. Dash

Parsley (optional)

What I Use

small skillet with lid

1-cup measure

½-cup measure

¼-cup measure

wooden spoon

1-Tablespoon measure

timer

HEALTHY MEAL TIP

Serve **Golden Glazed Carrots** with **Turkey Rice Casserole** and **Florida Citrus Salad**.

What I Do

1. Wash my hands.

2. Place skillet on stove. Measure oil and pour in skillet.

3. Measure carrots. Add to skillet.

4. Turn heat to MEDIUM. Cook carrots until light brown, about 10 minutes. Stir every 2 to 3 minutes with wooden spoon.

5. Measure water. Carefully add to carrots.

6. Measure brown sugar. Add to carrots.

7. Shake seasoning on carrots.

8. Cover carrots with lid. Cook on LOW heat for 15 minutes. Use timer. Turn off stove. Add parsley, if desired.

Serve and ENJOY!

Lettuce & Tomato Salad

Number of Servings

This recipe makes 2 servings
1 serving = 1 salad

Meal Planning

Vegetables

What I Need

6   lettuce leaves

2   tomatoes

2   Tablespoons fat-free salad dressing

What I Use

2 salad bowls

cutting board

sharp knife

1-Tablespoon measure

2 paper towels

HEALTHY MEAL TIP

Serve **Lettuce & Tomato Salad** with **Western Skillet** and chocolate pudding.

What I Do

1.  Wash my hands.

2. Remove 6 lettuce leaves from head of lettuce.

3. Rinse lettuce leaves under cold running water. Place lettuce leaves on a paper towel. Place another paper towel on top and pat lightly.

4. Rinse tomatoes under cold running water.

5. On a cutting board, cut each tomato into 4 pieces with sharp knife.

6. With hands, break lettuce into bite-size pieces. Put half in one bowl and half in the other bowl.

7. Place 4 tomato wedges on top of each salad.

8. Measure 1 Tablespoon salad dressing. Pour over each salad.

Serve and ENJOY!

Microwave Vegetables

Number of Servings

This recipe makes 1 serving
1 serving = ½ cup

Meal Planning

Vegetables

What I Need

½ cup frozen vegetables (plain or combination)

1 Tablespoon water

1 Tablespoon soft-tub margarine

Dash of black pepper or salt-free seasoning blend (optional)

What I Use

small microwave-safe glass bowl

½-cup measure

fork

1-Tablespoon measure

clear plastic wrap or paper towel

oven mitts

HEALTHY MEAL TIP

Serve **Microwave Vegetables** with **Meatloaf** and a **Baked Potato**. Enjoy fresh fruit for dessert.

What I Do

1. Wash my hands.

2. Measure vegetables. Pour in bowl. Seal bag of leftover vegetables. Put back in freezer.

3. Measure and add water to bowl. Cover bowl with clear plastic wrap or paper towel.

4. Place glass bowl in the microwave. Cook for 3 minutes on MEDIUM POWER.

5. Remove bowl from microwave using oven mitts. Remove plastic wrap.

6. Measure margarine. Place on top vegetables.

7. Test vegetables with fork. If tender, yet crunchy, they are done. If vegetables are too hard, return to microwave for 30 seconds more.

8. Shake in pepper, your favorite salt-free seasoning, or eat plain.

Serve and ENJOY!

Speedy Tossed Salad

Number of Servings

This recipe makes 2 servings
1 serving = 1 cup

Meal Planning

Vegetables

What I Need

1½ cups lettuce greens (prepackaged, bite-size pieces)

1   small green bell pepper (½ cup chopped)

6   cherry tomatoes

½   cup shredded carrots (prepackaged)

2   Tablespoons raspberry vinaigrette dressing

What I Use

salad bowl

strainer

cutting board

sharp knife

1-cup measure

½-cup measure

fork and spoon

1-Tablespoon measure

paper towels

clear plastic wrap

HEALTHY MEAL TIP

Serve **Speedy Tossed Salad** with **Chili Macaroni** and **Yogurt & Fruit Parfait**.

What I Do

1. Wash my hands.

   Place strainer in sink.

2. Measure lettuce. Place in strainer.

3. Rinse lettuce under cold running water. Use paper towels to pat lettuce dry. Add lettuce to salad bowl.

4. Place bell pepper and cherry tomatoes in strainer. Rinse under cold running water.

5. On cutting board, cut bell pepper in half with a sharp knife. Remove stem and seeds and throw in thrash. Chop bell pepper to fill ½-cup measure. Add to lettuce.

6. Wrap leftover bell pepper in plastic wrap. Place in fridge.

7. On cutting board, cut cherry tomatoes in half using sharp knife. Add to salad bowl.

8. Measure shredded carrots. Pour in strainer. Rinse under cold running water.

9. Measure and add carrots to salad bowl.

10. Add salad dressing.

11. Toss lettuce and dressing together using fork and spoon.

Serve and ENJOY!

Spinach Apple Salad

Number of Servings

This recipe makes 2 servings
1 serving = 1 salad

Meal Planning

Vegetables and fruits

What I Need

2   cups fresh baby spinach leaves

1   large apple

3   Tablespoons raspberry vinaigrette dressing

¼   cup dried cranberries

2   Tablespoons pecan halves (optional)

What I Use

2 salad plates

medium salad bowl

strainer

cutting board

sharp knife

1-cup and ¼-cup measures

fork and spoon

1-Tablespoon measure

paper towel

HEALTHY MEAL TIP

Serve **Spinach Apple Salad** with **Baked Salmon** and **Indian Rice**.

What I Do

1. Wash my hands.

   Place strainer in sink.

2. Measure spinach into strainer. Rinse under cold running water. Shake strainer to remove water.

3. Put spinach on paper towel to dry.

4. Wash apple. On cutting board, use sharp knife to cut apple in half and half again.

5. Remove core and throw in trash. Cut apple into bite-size pieces.

6. Measure vinaigrette dressing into salad bowl.

7. Add apple pieces to salad bowl.

8. Measure and add to salad bowl—
   - cranberries
   - pecans (if using)
   - spinach

9. Toss with fork and spoon. Be sure dressing is mixed well with salad.

10. Place half the salad on 1 salad plate and half on the other plate.

Serve and ENJOY!

Stir-Fry Zucchini

Number of Servings

This recipe makes 1 serving
1 serving = ½ cup

Meal Planning

Vegetables

What I Need

1   small zucchini

Nonstick cooking spray

1   Tablespoon water

¼   teaspoon lemon pepper

What I Use

medium skillet with lid

cutting board

sharp knife

wooden spoon

1-Tablespoon measure

¼-teaspoon measure

HEALTHY MEAL TIP

Serve **Stir-Fry Zucchini** with **Smothered Pork Chop** and fresh fruit.

What I Do

1. Wash my hands.

2. Rinse zucchini under cold running water.

3. On cutting board, slice zucchini in round shapes with sharp knife.

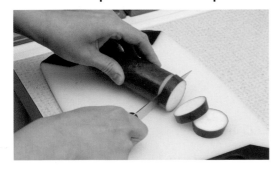

4. Spray skillet with cooking spray. Place skillet on stove.

5. Measure and add to skillet—
   • water
   • lemon pepper

6. Add zucchini rounds to skillet.

7. Put lid on skillet. Turn heat to MEDIUM.

8. Cook zucchini for 2 to 3 minutes. Stir with wooden spoon.

9. Turn off stove.

Serve and ENJOY!

Baked Potato

Number of Servings

This recipe makes 1 serving
1 serving = 1 potato

Meal Planning

Starchy vegetables

What I Need

1   medium potato
1   Tablespoon soft-tub margarine
2   Tablespoons fat-free sour cream

What I Use

microwave-safe plate

scrub brush or pad

fork

small knife

1-Tablespoon measure

paper towel

HEALTHY MEAL TIP

Serve **Baked Potato** with **Apricot Curry Chicken** and **Lettuce & Tomato Salad**.

What I Do

1. Wash my hands.

2. Scrub potato with scrub brush or pad under cold running water.

3. Use fork to poke holes in potato 3 or 4 times.

4. Place potato on plate. Cover with paper towel.

5. Microwave for 3 minutes on HIGH POWER. With fork, test potato. If it is hard, cook for 30 seconds more. Test again. If still not soft, return to microwave. When fork or knife goes in easily, potato is done.

6. Allow potato to cool for 2 to 3 minutes.

7. Cut open top of potato with small knife.

8. Measure margarine, put on top of cut potato.

9. Measure and add fat-free sour cream.

Serve and ENJOY!

Confetti Corn

Number of Servings

This recipe makes 4 servings
1 serving = ½ cup

Meal Planning

Starchy vegetables

What I Need

Nonstick cooking spray

1 egg

1 (15-ounce) can reduced-sodium whole-kernel corn

2 Tablespoons soft-tub margarine

2 Tablespoons pimento (½ of a 2-ounce jar)

Dash of black pepper

1½ ounces crispy fried onion (½ of a 2.8-ounce can)

What I Use

small baking dish with lid

strainer

small mixing bowl

can opener

fork

wooden spoon

1-Tablespoon measure

timer

oven mitt and pot holder

HEALTHY MEAL TIP

Serve **Confetti Corn** with **Turkey Burger** and **Apple Grape Salad**. Enjoy a small glass of cold low-fat milk.

What I Do

1. Wash my hands.

    Preheat oven to 325°F. Spray baking dish with cooking spray.

    Place strainer in sink.

2. Break egg in bowl. Throw shells in trash.

    Wash my hands.

3. Beat egg with fork until bubbly. Set aside.

4. Open corn with can opener. Pour corn into strainer to drain.

5. Place baking dish near sink. Pour corn into baking dish.

6. Add to corn and mix with wooden spoon—
   - egg
   - pimento
   - margarine
   - pepper

7. Shake fried onions on top.

8. Cover baking dish with lid. Place in oven.

    Set timer for 35 minutes.

9. When timer goes off, turn off oven. Carefully remove from oven with oven mitt and pot holder.

Serve and ENJOY!

Corn Chowder

Number of Servings

This recipe makes 6 servings
1 serving = 1 cup

Meal Planning

Starchy vegetables and dairy

What I Need

1   Tablespoon soft-tub margarine

½   cup chopped frozen or fresh onion

½   cup water

1   (16-ounce) bag frozen hash brown potatoes

1   (15-ounce) can cream-style corn

2   cups skim milk

What I Use

large 4-quart pot

can opener

1-cup and ½-cup measures

wooden spoon

1-Tablespoon measure

timer

cutting board and sharp knife (for fresh onion)

HEALTHY MEAL TIP

Serve **Corn Chowder** with **Fish Sandwich** and fresh fruit.

What I Do

1. Wash my hands.

2. If using fresh onion: On cutting board, chop onion into small pieces with sharp knife.

3. Place pot on stove. Measure and add to pot—
   • margarine   • onion

4. Cook on MEDIUM heat until onion is soft. Stir every 2 to 3 minutes with wooden spoon.

5. Measure water. Pour into pot.

6. Open bag of hash brown potatoes. Pour all the potatoes into pot. Stir.

7.  Set timer for 10 minutes. Cook on MEDIUM heat.

8. When timer goes off, open creamed corn. Use spoon to scrape corn into pot.

9. Measure milk. Pour into pot. Stir well.

10. Set timer for 10 minutes. Cook on LOW heat.

11. Stir every 2 to 3 minutes with wooden spoon. Do not boil. When timer goes off, turn off stove.

Serve and ENJOY!

Gingered Sweet Potatoes

Number of Servings

This recipe makes 1 serving
1 serving = 1 potato

Meal Planning

Starchy vegetables

What I Need

1	small sweet potato (or half large)
2	teaspoons brown sugar
¼	teaspoon ground cinnamon
¼	teaspoon ground ginger

What I Use

small microwave-safe glass bowl

vegetable peeler

cutting board and sharp knife

spoon

1-teaspoon measure

¼-teaspoon measure

clear plastic wrap

HEALTHY MEAL TIP

Serve **Gingered Sweet Potatoes** with **Baked Chicken** and **Florida Citrus Salad**.

What I Do

1. Wash my hands.

2. Use vegetable peeler to peel skin from sweet potato.

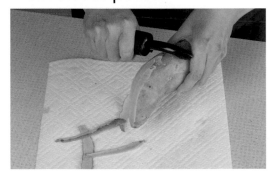

3. Rinse potato under cold running water.

4. On cutting board, cut potato in small cubes with sharp knife.

5. Pour cubes into bowl. Measure and shake brown sugar, cinnamon, and ginger on top of the cubes.

6. Cover bowl with clear plastic wrap.

7. Put bowl in microwave. Cook for 3 to 4 minutes on HIGH POWER.

8. Stir potato well with a spoon.

Serve and ENJOY!

Mashed Potatoes & Carrots

Number of Servings

This recipe makes 1 serving
1 serving = ½ cup

Meal Planning

Starchy vegetables

What I Need

2   small canned whole potatoes (no skin)

4   small baby carrots (prepackaged)

2   Tablespoons skim milk

¼   teaspoon dill weed

¼   teaspoon onion powder

What I Use

small microwave-safe glass bowl

can opener

fork

1-Tablespoon measure

¼-teaspoon measure

small storage container with lid

clear plastic wrap

oven mitts

HEALTHY MEAL TIP

Serve **Mashed Potatoes & Carrots** with **Meat Loaf** and **Sunflower Salad**.

What I Do

1.  Wash my hands.

2. Open can of potatoes with can opener.

3. Place 2 potatoes in microwave-safe bowl.

4. Pour leftover potatoes into storage container. Seal with lid. Label. Place in fridge.

5. Count out 4 small carrots. Add to potatoes.

6. Cover bowl with plastic wrap. Microwave for 3 to 4 minutes on HIGH POWER.

7. Remove bowl from microwave using oven mitts. Mash carrots and potatoes together with fork.

8. Measure and add to bowl—
   - skim milk
   - dill weed
   - onion powder

9. Mash with fork. Mix again.

10. Cover with plastic wrap.

11. Microwave for 30 seconds on HIGH POWER.

12. Remove bowl with oven mitts and mix well with fork.

Serve and ENJOY!

Pea Salad

Number of Servings

This recipe makes 4 servings
1 serving = ½ cup

Meal Planning

Starchy vegetables

What I Need

1½ cups frozen peas

½   cup chopped frozen or fresh onion

1   (6-ounce) container plain low-fat yogurt

¼   cup light mayonnaise

½   teaspoon dill weed

Dash of black pepper or salt-free herb blend

What I Use

medium mixing bowl

strainer

1-cup measure

½-cup measure

¼-cup measure

spatula

½-teaspoon measure

cutting board and sharp knife (for fresh onion)

HEALTHY MEAL TIP

Serve **Pea Salad** with **Baked Salmon** and **Indian Rice**.

What I Do

1. Wash my hands.

   Place strainer in sink.

2. If using fresh onion: On cutting board, chop onion into small pieces with sharp knife.

3. Measure peas and onions, if frozen, into strainer. Run warm water over peas and onions to thaw.

4. Stir to break apart with spatula. Let sit in sink until thawed and well drained.

5. Use spatula to pour yogurt into mixing bowl. Measure mayonnaise. Add to yogurt.

6. Measure dill weed. Add to mixing bowl with yogurt and mayonnaise. Stir well with spatula.

7. Add well-drained peas and onions to bowl. Stir gently with spatula.

8. Stir salad to cover all peas and onions with dressing.

9. Shake in pepper or salt-free herb blend.

Serve and ENJOY!

Super Spud

Number of Servings

This recipe makes 3 servings
1 serving = 1 potato

Meal Planning

Starchy vegetables and dairy

What I Need

3	medium potatoes
1	(10.75-ounce) can reduced-sodium, low-fat cheddar cheese soup
¼	cup skim milk
1	(10-ounce) bag frozen chopped broccoli
3	Tablespoons bacon bits

What I Use

glass pie plate

small mixing bowl

medium microwave-safe glass bowl

scrub brush or pad

¼-cup and ½-cup measures

fork, spoon, spatula, and sharp knife

1-Tablespoon measure

2 paper towels

oven mitt and pot holder

small storage container with lid

HEALTHY MEAL TIP

Serve **Super Spud** with **Pork Chop Apple Bake** and **Florida Citrus Salad**.

What I Do

1. Wash my hands.

2. Scrub potatoes well with scrub brush under cold running water. Use a fork to poke holes 3 or 4 times in each potato.

3. Place potatoes on glass pie plate. Cover with a paper towel.

4. Microwave 6 to 9 minutes on HIGH POWER. With fork, test the potatoes. If they are hard, cook another minute.

5. Open soup. Pour into small mixing bowl. Measure milk. Add to soup. Stir with spatula.

6. Open broccoli. Pour into medium glass bowl.

7. Pour soup over broccoli. Mix well. Cover bowl with new paper towel.

8. Place cheese-broccoli mixture into microwave. Cook for 3 to 5 minutes on HIGH POWER.

    Wash my hands.

9. Remove from microwave with oven mitt and pot holder. Let rest for 1 minute.

10. Use an oven mitt to put a potato on each serving plate. With sharp knife cut open each potato.

11. Spoon ½ cup of cheese-broccoli mixture on top of each potato.

12. Add bacon bits.

13. Put leftover cheese-broccoli mixture in storage container. Seal with lid. Label. Place in fridge.

     Wash my hands.

Serve and ENJOY!

Apple Grape Salad

Number of Servings

This recipe makes 3 servings
1 serving = ¾ cup

Meal Planning

Fruits

What I Need

1	large apple
15	grapes
¼	cup raisins
¼	cup chopped walnuts
1	Tablespoon light mayonnaise

What I Use

medium bowl

strainer

cutting board

sharp knife

¼-cup measure

spatula

1-Tablespoon measure

HEALTHY MEAL TIP

Serve **Apple Grape Salad** with **Chinese Pork** and **Instant Brown Rice**. Enjoy a small glass of cold lowfat milk.

What I Do

1. Wash my hands.

   Place strainer in sink.

2. Place apple and grapes in strainer. Rinse under cold running water.

3. Place apple on cutting board and cut into 4 pieces with sharp knife.

4. Cut core off apple pieces. Throw away core.

5. Cut apple into small pieces and add to bowl.

6. Take grapes off stems. Put grapes in bowl with apple pieces. Throw away stems.

7. Measure and add to bowl—
   - raisins
   - walnuts
   - mayonnaise

8. Mix gently with spatula until well blended.

Place in fridge to keep cold.

Serve and ENJOY!

Apple Slaw

Number of Servings

This recipe makes 3 servings
1 serving = ¾ cup

Meal Planning

Fruits and vegetables

What I Need

Dressing

2 Tablespoons raisins

1 Tablespoon vinegar

½ teaspoon dry mustard

½ cup plain low-fat yogurt

Coleslaw

1½ cups coleslaw or shredded
cabbage (prepackaged)

1 medium apple

1 celery rib (¼ cup chopped)

What I Use

salad bowl	½-cup measure
small bowl	¼-cup measure
strainer	spatula
cutting board	1-Tablespoon
sharp knife	measure
paper towel	½-teaspoon
1-cup measure	measure

HEALTHY MEAL TIP

Serve **Apple Slaw** with **Meat Loaf**,
Confetti Corn and whole wheat bun.

What I Do

1. Wash my hands.

   Place strainer in sink.

For Dressing

2. Measure and add to small bowl—
   - raisins
   - mustard
   - yogurt
   - vinegar

   Mix well.

3. Place dressing in fridge to chill.

For Slaw

4. Measure cabbage. Put in strainer. Rinse cabbage under cold running water.

5. Pour cabbage into salad bowl. Press paper towel on cabbage to dry.

6. Rinse apple and celery under cold running water. Check to remove all dirt.

7. On cutting board, use sharp knife to cut apple in half, then half again to make 4 pieces. Cut core off apple pieces and throw away.

8. Chop apple in smaller pieces. Add apple to salad bowl.

9. On cutting board, cut celery in small pieces. Add to bowl.

10. Add dressing from fridge. Mix well. Place salad in fridge until mealtime.

Serve and ENJOY!

Baked Apple

Number of Servings

This recipe makes 1 serving
1 serving = 1 apple

Meal Planning

Fruits

What I Need

1	small apple
2	Tablespoons water
1	teaspoon soft-tub margarine
1	teaspoon sugar
¼	teaspoon ground cinnamon
1	Tablespoon raisins

What I Use

small baking dish

small mixing bowl

cutting board

sharp knife

measuring spoons

spatula

timer

oven mitt and pot holder

HEALTHY MEAL TIP

Serve **Baked Apple** with **Chili Macaroni** and **Speedy Tossed Salad**.

What I Do

1. Wash my hands.

    Preheat oven to 375°F.

2. Rinse apple under cold running water.

3. On cutting board, cut apple in 4 pieces with sharp knife. Cut core off apple pieces and throw core away.

4. Place apples in baking dish with skin side up.

5. Measure and pour into mixing bowl—
   - water
   - raisins
   - sugar
   - margarine
   - cinnamon

6. Mix well with spatula. Pour over apples in baking dish.

7.  Bake apples in oven uncovered for 30 minutes. Set timer.

8. When timer goes off, turn off oven. Remove dish from oven with oven mitt and pot holder.

9. Wait 5 minutes for apples to cool.

Serve and ENJOY!

Florida Citrus Salad

Number of Servings

This recipe makes 3 servings
1 serving = ¾ cup

Meal Planning

Fruits and vegetables

What I Need

4	lettuce leaves
1	(15-ounce) can citrus fruit (red and white grapefruit or grapefruit and oranges)
2	Tablespoons peach or vanilla low-fat yogurt

What I Use

salad bowl

strainer

can opener

wooden spoon

1-Tablespoon measure

paper towel

HEALTHY MEAL TIP

Serve **Florida Citrus Salad** with **Baked Chicken** and **Gingered Sweet Potato**.

FRUITS

What I Do

1. Wash my hands.

Place strainer in sink.

2. Take 4 lettuce leaves from head of lettuce. Put lettuce leaves into strainer. Rinse lettuce under cold running water.

3. Place lettuce on paper towel to dry.

4. Open can of fruit with can opener. Pour fruit into strainer to drain.

5. Break lettuce into small pieces. Add to salad bowl.

6. Measure yogurt. Add yogurt to lettuce pieces in bowl.

7. Pour fruit in bowl.

8. Mix salad gently with wooden spoon.

Serve and ENJOY!

Pineapple Cabbage Salad

Number of Servings

This recipe makes 3 servings
1 serving = 1 cup

Meal Planning

Fruits and vegetables

What I Need

Salad

1½ cups shredded cabbage
    (prepackaged)

1   small apple

¼   cup raisins

1   (8-ounce) can crushed pineapple

Dressing

3   Tablespoons plain low-fat yogurt

2   Tablespoons ketchup

What I Use

salad bowl

strainer

small mixing bowl

can opener

cutting board and sharp knife

1-cup, ½-cup, and ¼-cup measures

spatula

fork

1-Tablespoon measure

paper towel

HEALTHY MEAL TIP

Serve **Pineapple Cabbage Salad** with **Baked Salmon** and **Baked Potato**.

What I Do

1. Wash my hands.

 Place strainer in sink.

For Salad

2. Measure cabbage. Pour in strainer. Rinse cabbage under cold running water. Press paper towel on cabbage to dry.

3. Pour cabbage into salad bowl.

4. Rinse apple under cold running water.

5. On cutting board, cut apple in 4 pieces with sharp knife. Cut core off apple pieces and throw core away.

6. Chop apple in small pieces. Add apple to bowl with cabbage.

7. Measure raisins. Add raisins to bowl.

8. Open crushed pineapple with can opener. Do not drain. Add to bowl with fork.

For Dressing

9. Measure yogurt and ketchup together in small bowl.

10. Stir dressing with spatula.

11. Add dressing to salad bowl.

12. Mix well. Place bowl in fridge to chill.

Serve and ENJOY!

Pineapple Carrot Salad

Number of Servings

This recipe makes 2 servings
1 serving = 1 salad

Meal Planning

Fruits and vegetables

What I Need

2   large lettuce leaves

1   (8-ounce) can pineapple slices

½   cup shredded carrots (prepackaged)

¼   cup raisins

¼   cup pineapple or orange low-fat yogurt

What I Use

2 salad plates

strainer

small mixing bowl

can opener

½-cup and ¼-cup measures

mixing spoon

fork

small storage container with lid

paper towel

HEALTHY MEAL TIP

Serve **Pineapple Carrot Salad** with **Turkey Burger** on whole wheat bun and a small glass of low-fat milk.

What I Do

1. Wash my hands.

    Place strainer in sink.

2. Place lettuce leaves in strainer. Rinse lettuce with cold running water.

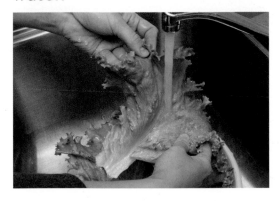

3. Press paper towel on lettuce to dry.

4. Place one lettuce leaf on first plate and one on second plate.

5. Open pineapple with can opener.

6. With fork, place one pineapple slice on top of lettuce on each plate.

7. Pour leftover pineapple into storage container. Cover with lid. Label. Place in fridge.

8. Measure and add to mixing bowl—
   - carrots
   - raisins
   - yogurt

9. Mix well. Spoon carrot mixture on top of each pineapple slice.

10. Place plates in fridge until ready to eat.

Serve and ENJOY!

Broccoli Cheese Soup

Number of Servings

This recipe makes 5 servings
1 serving = 1 cup

Meal Planning

Dairy and vegetables

What I Need

1   Tablespoon soft-tub margarine

3   Tablespoons chopped frozen or
    fresh onion

1   (10.75-ounce) can reduced-
    sodium, low-fat cream of chicken
    soup

1   cup shredded part-skim mozzarella
    cheese

1   cup shredded cheddar cheese

3   cups skim milk

1   (10-ounce) bag frozen chopped
    broccoli

What I Use

large 4-quart pot

can opener

1-cup measure

wooden spoon and spatula

1-Tablespoon measure

timer

cutting board (for fresh onion)

sharp knife (for fresh onion)

HEALTHY MEAL TIP

Serve **Broccoli Cheese Soup** with
Tuna Burger and a crisp juicy apple.
Enjoy a glass of cold water.

What I Do

1. Wash my hands.

2. If using fresh onion: On cutting board, chop onion into small pieces with sharp knife.

3. Place pot on stove. Set stove to LOW heat.

4. Measure margarine, add to pot. Let it melt.

5. Measure onion and add to pot.

6. With wooden spoon, cook and stir onion until soft.

7. Open soup with can opener. Pour soup into pot.

8. Use spatula to scrape all the soup out of can. Stir well.

9. Measure mozzarella and cheddar. Add to pot. Stir well.

10. Measure milk. Pour into pot.

11. Pour broccoli into pot. Stir well.

12.  Set timer for 15 minutes.

13. Use wooden spoon to mix until smooth. Continue to cook on LOW heat. (Do not boil.)

14. When timer goes off, turn off stove.

Serve and ENJOY!

Cottage Cheese Tomato Salad

Number of Servings

This recipe makes 1 serving
1 serving = 1 tomato salad

Meal Planning

Dairy and vegetables

What I Need

1   small tomato

½   cup low-fat cottage cheese

     Dash of black pepper or sunflower seeds

What I Use

serving plate

cutting board

sharp knife

spatula

½-cup measure

HEALTHY MEAL TIP

Serve **Cottage Cheese Tomato Salad** with a whole grain bun and a dish of fresh fruit.

What I Do

1. Wash my hands.

2. Rinse tomato under cold running water.

3. On cutting board, use sharp knife to slice tomato in half.

4. Slice each half tomato into 4 or 5 pieces.

5. I will have 8 to 10 pieces of tomato when I'm done.

6. Arrange tomato pieces on plate. Leave center open.

    Wash my hands.

7. Measure cottage cheese. Pour in center of tomato pieces.

8. Shake pepper (or sunflower seeds) on top of cottage cheese.

Serve and ENJOY!

Easy Cheese Quesadilla

Number of Servings

This recipe makes 1 serving
1 serving = 1 quesadilla

Meal Planning

Dairy and grains

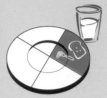

What I Need

Nonstick cooking spray

2   (6-inch) whole wheat tortillas

⅓   cup shredded Mexican-style cheese

3   Tablespoons canned diced
     tomatoes with green chiles

1   Tablespoon fat-free sour cream

What I Use

cookie sheet

serving plate

can opener

⅓-cup measure

spatula and knife

1-Tablespoon measure

timer

oven mitt and pot holder

small storage container with lid

HEALTHY MEAL TIP

Serve **Easy Cheese Quesadilla** as a
snack, or as a meal with **Tuna Apple
Salad** and fresh vegetable sticks.

What I Do

1. Wash my hands.

   Preheat oven to 325°F.

2. Spray cookie sheet with cooking spray. Lay 1 tortilla on cookie sheet.

3. Measure ⅓ cup shredded cheese. Spread on tortilla.

4. Open can of tomatoes with can opener. Measure tomatoes and sprinkle over cheese.

5. Use spatula to scrape leftover tomatoes into storage container. Cover with lid. Label. Place in fridge.

6. Place second tortilla on top of cheese and tomatoes. It's like making a sandwich.

7. Put cookie sheet in oven.

    Set timer for 10 minutes.

8. When timer goes off, remove cookie sheet with oven mitt and pot holder. Turn off oven.

9. Place quesadilla on serving plate. With sharp knife, cut quesadilla like a pizza.

10. Measure and put sour cream on plate.

Serve and ENJOY!

Fruit Smoothie

Number of Servings

This recipe makes 1 serving

1 serving = 1 smoothie

Meal Planning

Dairy and fruits

What I Need

4   large frozen strawberries

1   small banana

1   (6-ounce) container low-fat vanilla yogurt

What I Use

blender

12-ounce glass

spatula

storage container with lid

HEALTHY MEAL TIP

Serve **Fruit Smoothie** as a snack, or as a meal with a **Tuna Burger** and fresh vegetable sticks.

What I Do

1. Wash my hands.

2. Count out 4 frozen strawberries. Put berries into blender.

3. Pour leftover strawberries into storage container. Seal with lid. Label. Place in freezer.

4. Peel banana. Place banana in blender. Throw peel in trash.

    Wash my hands.

5. Use spatula to pour yogurt into blender. It will look like this.

6. Put lid on blender. Blend for 2 minutes.

7. Turn off blender. Use rubber spatula to mix. Remove the spatula.

8. Place lid on blender. Blend for 1 minute more.

9. Pour smoothie into large glass.

Serve and ENJOY!

Sunflower Salad

Number of Servings

This recipe makes 1 serving
1 serving = 1 salad

Meal Planning

Dairy and fruits

What I Need

5   canned peach slices

⅓   cup low-fat cottage cheese

1   Tablespoon light mayonnaise

2   Tablespoons raisins

What I Use

small plate and serving plate

small mixing bowl

can opener

⅓-cup measure

spatula

fork

1-Tablespoon measure

small storage container with lid

HEALTHY MEAL TIP

Serve **Sunflower Salad** with **Chili**.
Enjoy a glass of cold water.

What I Do

1. Wash my hands.

2. Open peaches with can opener. With fork, remove 5 peach slices from can; put on small plate. Set aside.

3. Pour leftover peaches and juice into storage container with lid. Label. Place in fridge.

4. Measure cottage cheese. Put in bowl.

5. Measure mayonnaise. Add to bowl with cottage cheese.

6. Mix well with spatula.

7. Use the same spatula to spoon cottage cheese into center of serving plate.

8. With fork, arrange peach slices around cottage cheese to look like petals on a sunflower.

9. Measure raisins. Sprinkle on top of cottage cheese to look like sunflower seeds.

 Wash my hands.

10. Place salad in fridge until ready to eat.

Serve and ENJOY!

Yogurt & Fruit Parfait

Number of Servings

This recipe makes 1 serving
1 serving = 1 parfait

Meal Planning

Dairy and fruits

What I Need

½ cup fresh or frozen blueberries or strawberries, plus 2 or 3 for topping

1 (6-ounce) container low-fat vanilla yogurt

2 Tablespoons granola or cornflake cereal

What I Use

8-ounce glass

½-cup measure

spoon

1-Tablespoon measure

HEALTHY MEAL TIP

Serve **Yogurt & Fruit Parfait** with **Chili Macaroni** and **Speedy Tossed Salad**.

What I Do

1. 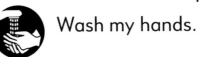 Wash my hands.

2. Measure berries. Pour half in glass.

3. Spoon half the yogurt on top of berries.

4. Pour rest of berries on top of yogurt.

5. Spoon rest of yogurt on top of berries.

6. Measure granola. Shake over yogurt.

7. Add 2 or 3 berries to top of parfait. Wash my hands.

Serve and ENJOY!

French Toast & Breakfast Links

Number of Servings

This recipe makes 1 serving
1 serving = 2 slices French toast and 2 links

Meal Planning

Protein and grains

What I Need

2   vegetarian or low-fat turkey breakfast links

1   egg

½   teaspoon ground cinnamon (optional)

⅓   cup low-fat milk

1   teaspoon soft-tub margarine

2   slices whole wheat bread

What I Use

serving plate

medium skillet

small mixing bowl

pie plate

microwave-safe plate

⅓-cup measure

fork and small wire whisk

1-teaspoon measure

turner

paper towel

HEALTHY MEAL TIP

Serve **French Toast & Breakfast Links** with low-sugar maple syrup and fresh berries.

What I Do

For Breakfast Links

1. Wash my hands.

2. Place 2 links on microwave-safe plate. Cover with paper towel.

3. Microwave on HIGH POWER for 45 seconds. With fork, turn links over. Microwave on HIGH for 30 seconds. Set aside.

For French Toast

4. Wash my hands.

5. Break egg in mixing bowl. Throw shells in trash.

 Wash my hands.

6. Use fork to mix egg until bubbly. Measure and add cinnamon, if desired. Mix well.

7. Measure milk. Add to egg. Beat well.

8. Pour egg-milk mixture into pie plate.

9. Place skillet on stove. Measure and melt margarine in skillet on LOW heat.

10. Place a slice of bread in pie plate to soak up egg-milk mixture. Turn slice of bread over to other side. Use turner to lift bread into skillet.

 Wash my hands.

11. Cook each side for 3 to 5 minutes on MEDIUM heat. Place on plate with turner.

12. Repeat with second slice of bread. Turn off stove.

Serve with links and ENJOY!

Veggie Omelet

Number of Servings

This recipe makes 1 serving
1 serving = 1 omelet

Meal Planning

Protein

What I Need

2   Tablespoons frozen or fresh broccoli florets

2   Tablespoons frozen or fresh chopped onion

1   large egg

1   Tablespoon low-fat milk

    Dash of salt and black pepper

2   Tablespoons shredded cheddar cheese

Nonstick cooking spray

What I Use

serving plate

small skillet

small microwave-safe glass bowl

small mixing bowl

fork

1-Tablespoon measure

turner

clear plastic wrap

cutting board (for fresh onion)

sharp knife (for fresh onion)

HEALTHY MEAL TIP

Serve **Veggie Omelet** with whole wheat toast and fresh orange wedges.

What I Do

1. Wash my hands.

2. If using fresh onion: On cutting board, chop onion into small pieces with sharp knife.

3. Measure broccoli and onion into glass bowl. Cover with plastic wrap.

4. Put vegetables in microwave for 30 seconds on DEFROST or LOW POWER. Remove and set aside.

5. Break egg into small mixing bowl. Throw shells in trash.

    Wash my hands.

6. Use fork to beat egg until bubbly.

7. Measure and add to beaten egg—
   - milk
   - vegetables
   - salt and pepper
   - cheddar

8. Stir lightly with fork.

9. Place skillet on stove. Spray skillet with nonstick cooking spray.

10. Pour egg mixture into skillet. Turn stove to MEDIUM heat.

11. Use turner to stir eggs gently. When eggs look cooked, not runny, turn eggs over with turner. Cook for another 2 to 3 minutes on MEDIUM heat.

12. With turner, lift the omelet and fold in half.

13. Carefully pick up skillet and slide omelet onto plate. Turn off stove.

     Wash my hands.

Serve and ENJOY!

Baked Salmon

Number of Servings

This recipe makes 2 servings (palm size).
1 serving = 3 ounces

Meal Planning

Protein

What I Need

½   pound (8 ounces) fresh salmon

1   lemon

½   teaspoon dill weed

Dash of salt and black pepper

What I Use

7 × 11-inch glass baking dish

cutting board

sharp knife

½-teaspoon measure

aluminum foil

timer

oven mitt and pot holder

HEALTHY MEAL TIP

Serve **Baked Salmon** with **Indian Rice** and **Spinach Apple Salad**.

What I Do

1. Wash my hands.

   Preheat oven to 425°F.

2. Cut a large piece of foil to cover the bottom and sides of baking dish.

3. Unwrap salmon. Place salmon in baking dish.

    Wash my hands.

4. Wash lemon under cold running water. On cutting board, use sharp knife to cut lemon in half. Cut each half again to make 4 wedges.

5. Squeeze 2 lemon wedges over salmon.

6. Lay wedges on top of salmon. Save other lemon wedges for later.

    Wash my hands.

7. Measure and shake dill weed on salmon.

8. Cover salmon with foil.
    Bake covered for 20 minutes. Use timer.

9. With oven mitt and pot holder, carefully remove baking dish from oven. Turn off oven.

10. Cut salmon in 2 pieces. Serve on 2 plates. Place a fresh wedge of lemon on top of salmon.

     Wash my hands.

Serve and ENJOY!

Fish Sandwich

Number of Servings

This recipe makes 1 serving
1 serving = 1 fish sandwich (palm size)

Meal Planning

Protein, grains, and dairy

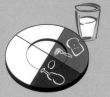 

What I Need

1   frozen fish fillet patty
    (any unbreaded fish square)

1   slice American cheese

1   whole wheat hamburger bun

1   Tablespoon tartar sauce

    Lettuce leaf

What I Use

serving plate

cookie sheet

1-Tablespoon
measure

turner and table
knife

aluminum foil

timer

oven mitt and pot
holder

food thermometer

HEALTHY MEAL TIP

Serve **Fish Sandwich** with **Corn Chowder** and fresh fruit.

What I Do

1. Wash my hands.

   Preheat oven to 400°F.

2. Cut a piece of foil to cover bottom of cookie sheet. Place fish square on cookie sheet.

   Set timer for 20 minutes. Bake fish.

3. When timer goes off, use oven mitt and pot holder to carefully remove cookie sheet from oven.

4. Unwrap cheese slice. Place cheese slice on top of fish. Put fish back in oven.

   Set timer for 2 minutes.

5. When timer goes off, use oven mitt and pot holder to carefully remove cookie sheet from oven. Use food thermometer (see pages 12, 16). Turn off oven.

6. Open hamburger bun and place on plate.

7. Measure tartar sauce. Use table knife to spread sauce on bun.

8. Use turner to lift fish patty onto bun.

9. Add lettuce leaf to my sandwich.

 Wash my hands.

Serve and ENJOY!

Tuna Apple Salad

Number of Servings

This recipe makes 2 servings
1 serving = ¾ cup

Meal Planning

Protein and fruits

What I Need

1   large apple
1   lettuce leaf
1   (5-ounce) can tuna, in water
2   Tablespoons light mayonnaise

What I Use

serving plate

small mixing bowl

strainer

can opener

cutting board and
sharp knife

1-Tablespoon
measure

mixing spoon

paper towels

HEALTHY MEAL TIP

Serve **Tuna Apple Salad** with a
fresh whole grain bun and fresh
vegetable sticks and blueberries.
Enjoy a small glass of low-fat milk.

What I Do

1.  Wash my hands.

 Put strainer in sink.

2. Rinse apple and lettuce leaf under cold running water. Set aside on paper towels to dry.

3. Open can of tuna with can opener. Empty tuna into strainer to drain water.

4. With spoon, put all tuna in small bowl.

5. On cutting board, cut apple into small pieces with sharp knife. Remove and throw away core.

6. Add apple to tuna in bowl.

7. Measure mayonnaise and add to bowl. Mix well with spoon.

 Wash my hands.

8. Place lettuce leaf on plate. Spoon salad on lettuce leaf.

Serve and ENJOY!

Tuna Burger

Number of Servings

This recipe makes 2 servings
1 serving = 1 tuna burger

Meal Planning

Protein and grains

What I Need

1	celery rib (½ cup chopped)
2	green onions
1	(5-ounce) can tuna, in water
¼	cup shredded cheddar cheese
1	Tablespoon light mayonnaise
2	whole wheat hamburger buns

What I Use

cookie sheet

small mixing bowl

strainer and can opener

cutting board and sharp knife

¼-cup measure

mixing spoon

1-Tablespoon measure

aluminum foil

timer

oven mitt and pot holder

HEALTHY MEAL TIP

Serve **Tuna Burger** with **Fruit Smoothie** and fresh vegetable sticks.

What I Do

1. Wash my hands.

     Put strainer in sink.

     Preheat oven to 350°F.

2. Wash celery and onion under cold running water. Remove all dirt.

3. On cutting board, cut celery and onion into small pieces with sharp knife. Place in small bowl.

4. Open tuna with can opener. Empty tuna into strainer to drain.

5. With spoon, add tuna to bowl.

6. Measure cheese and mayonnaise and add to bowl. Mix well with spoon.

7. Cut 2 squares of aluminum foil. Place foil squares on cookie sheet. Lay bottom of each bun on foil square.

8. Use spoon to fill each bun with tuna.

9. Put top of each bun on tuna. Wrap foil square around each bun.

     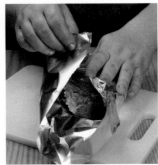

10. Put cookie sheet in oven.

     Wash my hands.

     Set timer for 15 minutes.

11. When timer goes off, use oven mitt and pot holder to remove cookie sheet from oven. Turn off oven. Unwrap carefully.

Serve and ENJOY!

Tuna Pasta Salad

Number of Servings

This recipe makes 3 servings
1 serving = 1 cup

Meal Planning

Protein and grains

What I Need

4	cups water
1	cup whole wheat elbow macaroni (dry)
1	celery rib (½ cup chopped)
12	seedless red or green grapes
3	Tablespoons light mayonnaise
1	(5-ounce) can tuna, in water
	Dash of black pepper

What I Use

medium pot

strainer

medium mixing bowl

cutting board and sharp knife

can opener

1-cup measure

wooden spoon

1-Tablespoon measure

timer

clear plastic wrap

HEALTHY MEAL TIP

Serve **Tuna Pasta Salad** with **Golden Glazed Carrots** and watermelon wedges.

What I Do

1. Wash my hands.

   Place strainer in sink.

2. Measure and pour water into pot. Place pot on stove. Turn stove to HIGH until water boils.

3. Put macaroni in boiling water. Turn stove to MEDIUM heat.

   Set timer to 12 minutes. Cook macaroni.

4. Rinse celery under cold running water. Remove all dirt.

5. On cutting board, cut celery in small pieces with sharp knife. Put in bowl.

6. Rinse grapes under cold running water. Cut grapes in half on cutting board with sharp knife. Put grapes in bowl.

7. Measure mayonnaise. Add to bowl. Mix well with wooden spoon.

8. Open can of tuna with can opener. Pour tuna in strainer to drain water.

9. Add tuna to bowl. Place strainer back in sink.

10. When timer rings, turn off stove. Carefully pour water and macaroni into strainer to drain water. Rinse macaroni under cold running water.

11. Add macaroni to bowl.

12. Mix well with wooden spoon. Sprinkle with pepper.

     Wash my hands.

13. Cover bowl with plastic wrap. Place in fridge until mealtime.

Serve and ENJOY!

Apricot Curry Chicken

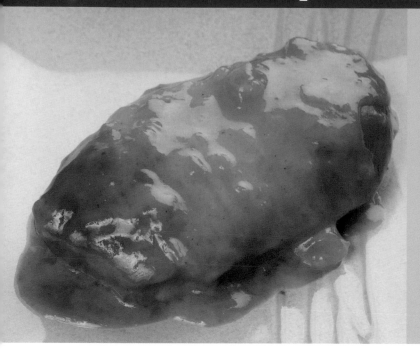

Number of Servings

This recipe makes 3 servings
1 serving = 1 chicken breast (palm size)

Meal Planning

Protein and fruits

What I Need

Nonstick cooking spray

3   boneless, skinless chicken breasts (about 4 ounces each)

1   (6-ounce) container low-fat plain yogurt

3   Tablespoons low-sugar apricot jam

¼   teaspoon curry powder

What I Use

glass baking dish (8 × 8-inch, 7 × 11-inch, or pie plate)

small mixing bowl

spoon

1-Tablespoon measure

¼-teaspoon measure

aluminum foil

timer

oven mitt and pot holder

food thermometer

HEALTHY MEAL TIP

Serve **Apricot Curry Chicken** with **Baked Potato** and **Speedy Tossed Salad**.

What I Do

1. Wash my hands.

    Preheat oven to 350°F. Spray baking dish with cooking spray

2. Remove chicken from wrapper. Place chicken in baking dish. Throw away meat wrapper.

    Wash my hands. Clean counter (see page 11).

3. Cover baking dish with aluminum foil. Put in oven.

    Set timer for 45 minutes. Make sauce while chicken bakes.

4. Measure and add to bowl—
   - yogurt
   - apricot jam
   - curry powder

   Mix well with spoon. Set aside.

5. When timer goes off, carefully remove baking dish from oven with oven mitt and pot holder. Carefully lift foil and remove.

6. Use food thermometer to test chicken. If less than 165°F, put chicken back in oven for another 10 minutes. Test again with food thermometer. If at (or above) 165°F, add sauce.

7. Pour sauce over chicken. Use spoon to spread sauce on top of chicken.

8. Put chicken back in oven, uncovered.

    Wash my hands.

    Set timer for 5 minutes.

9. When timer goes off, carefully remove baking dish from oven with oven mitt and pot holder. Turn off oven.

Serve and ENJOY!

Baked Chicken

Number of Servings

This recipe makes 3 servings
1 serving = 1 chicken breast (palm size)

Meal Planning

Protein

What I Need

Nonstick cooking spray

3 boneless, skinless chicken breasts (about 4 ounces each)

1 Tablespoon soft-tub margarine

2 Tablespoons dry onion soup mix

What I Use

glass baking dish (8 × 8-inch, 7 × 11-inch, or pie plate)

1-Tablespoon measure

aluminum foil

table knife

timer

oven mitt and pot holder

food thermometer

HEALTHY MEAL TIP

Serve **Baked Chicken** with **Gingered Sweet Potato** and **Florida Citrus Salad**.

What I Do

1. Wash my hands.

    Preheat oven to 350°F. Spray baking dish with cooking spray

2. Unwrap chicken. Place chicken in baking dish. Throw away meat wrapper.

    Wash my hands. Clean counter (see page 11).

3. Measure margarine. Spread margarine on top of chicken with table knife.

4. Measure and shake onion soup mix on top of chicken.

5. Cover chicken with foil. Put baking dish in oven.

    Set timer for 1 hour.

6. When timer goes off, take chicken out of oven using oven mitt and pot holder.

7. Put food thermometer into chicken. If 165°F or higher, chicken is ready to eat. If temperature is LESS than 165°F, cover chicken and put back into oven for another 15 minutes. Check chicken temperature again. Turn off oven if ready.

Serve and ENJOY!

Chicken Stir-Fry

Number of Servings

This recipe makes 3 servings
1 serving = 1 cup

Meal Planning

Protein and vegetables

What I Need

1	(12.5-ounce) can chicken pieces
1	Tablespoon olive oil
1	(10-ounce) bag frozen stir-fry vegetables
3	Tablespoons water
2	Tablespoons reduced-sodium soy sauce
½	teaspoon garlic powder
½	teaspoon onion powder
½	cup chow mein noodles

What I Use

3 serving plates

large skillet with lid

strainer

can opener and scissors

½-cup measure

wooden spoon

1-Tablespoon measure

½-teaspoon measure

timer

HEALTHY MEAL TIP

Serve **Chicken Stir-Fry** with **Instant Brown Rice** and sugar-free gelatin with fruit.

What I Do

1. Wash my hands.

    Place strainer in sink.

2. Open chicken with can opener. Pour chicken into strainer to drain.

3. Place skillet on stove. Turn stove to MEDIUM heat.

4. Measure oil. Add to skillet.

5. Open vegetable bag with scissors. Add all frozen vegetables to skillet. Stir with wooden spoon.

   Set timer for 6 minutes. Cook on MEDIUM heat. Stir twice.

6. Add chicken to skillet. Stir.

7. Measure and add to skillet—
   - water
   - soy sauce
   - garlic powder
   - onion powder

8. Stir well and cover.

9. Set timer for 5 minutes. Cook on MEDIUM heat. Stir every 2 minutes. Turn off stove.

10. Place chicken on each plate. Shake chow mein noodles on each serving.

     Wash my hands.

Serve and ENJOY!

Creamed Chicken over Rice

Number of Servings

This recipe makes 4 servings
1 serving = 1 cup creamed chicken over ½ cup rice

Meal Planning

Protein and grains

What I Need

1   recipe Instant Brown Rice, prepared (page 20)

2   celery ribs (1 cup chopped)

⅔   cup frozen or fresh chopped onion

1   pound boneless, skinless chicken breasts

1   (10.75-ounce) can reduced-sodium, low-fat cream of mushroom soup

2   Tablespoons olive oil

1   green onion, chopped

What I Use

4 serving plates

large skillet with lid

small microwave-safe glass bowl

can opener

cutting board

sharp knife

⅓-cup measure

wooden spoon

spatula

1-Tablespoon measure

timer

HEALTHY MEAL TIP

Serve **Creamed Chicken over Brown Rice** with **Spinach Apple Salad** and fruit (apricot halves pictured).

What I Do

1. Wash my hands.

2. Wash celery. Remove all dirt. On cutting board, cut celery and onion (if using fresh) into small pieces with sharp knife. Place in small bowl.

3. If using frozen onion: Measure and add onion to bowl. Set aside.

4. Unwrap chicken. Remove 1 chicken breast at a time to cutting board. Cut chicken into bite-size pieces with sharp knife.

 Throw away meat wrapper. Wash my hands. Clean counter (see page 11).

5. Measure and pour oil into skillet. Place skillet on stove. Turn stove to MEDIUM heat.

6. Add chicken to skillet.

 Wash my hands.

 Set timer for 7 minutes. When timer goes off, stir well.

7. Set timer for 7 more minutes. Stir. Chicken should look white, with no pink at all.

8. Add onion and celery to skillet. Cook for 5 minutes.

9. Open soup with can opener. Use spatula to scrape soup into skillet.

Cover skillet. Turn stove to LOW. Set timer for 15 minutes

10. When timer goes off, turn off stove.

11. Place cooked rice on plates. Top with chicken and green onion.

 Wash my hands.

Serve and ENJOY!

Turkey Burger

Number of Servings

This recipe makes 2 servings
1 serving = 3-ounce turkey burger with bun

Meal Planning

Protein and grains

What I Need

Nonstick cooking spray

¼ cup sliced fresh mushrooms, prepackaged

2 green onions

½ pound (8-ounces) extra lean ground turkey

1 Tablespoon dry onion soup mix

2 whole wheat hamburger buns

Mustard, pickles, lettuce, other condiments (optional)

What I Use

small skillet

medium mixing bowl

strainer

cutting board and sharp knife

¼-cup measure

fork and turner

1-Tablespoon measure

timer

food thermometer

HEALTHY MEAL TIP

Serve **Turkey Burger** with **Confetti Corn** and **Apple Grape Salad**. Enjoy a small glass of cold low-fat milk.

What I Do

1. Wash my hands.

    Place strainer in sink.

2. Spray skillet with cooking spray.

3. Measure mushrooms. Put in strainer. Add green onions to strainer. Rinse under cold running water.

4. On cutting board, cut green onions into small pieces with sharp knife.

5. Measure and add to bowl—
   - ground turkey
   - mushrooms
   - green onions
   - onion soup mix

6.  Throw away meat wrapper. Wash my hands. Clean counter (see page 11).

7. Mix well with fork.

8. Use hands to shape turkey into 2 patties. Place patties in skillet.

    Wash my hands.

    Place skillet on stove. Set timer for 5 minutes. Cook patties on MEDIUM heat.

9. When timer goes off, use turner to flip patty.

    Set timer for 6 minutes. Cook.

10. When timer goes off, press patty with turner. If juices are pink, cook for 4 more minutes. If juices are clear, turn off heat. Use food thermometer (see pages 12, 16).

     Wash my hands.

11. Use turner to place each patty on a bun bottom. Top each patty with mustard, pickle, and lettuce, if desired, and bun top.

Serve and ENJOY!

Turkey Rice Casserole

Number of Servings

This recipe makes 4 servings
1 serving = 1 cup

Meal Planning

Protein and grains

What I Need

1   recipe Instant Brown Rice, prepared (page 20)

½   cup sliced fresh mushrooms (prepackaged) or frozen peas

1   pound lean ground turkey

1   (10.5-ounce) can reduced-sodium cream of mushroom soup

2   Tablespoons dry onion soup mix

What I Use

large skillet with lid

strainer

can opener

½-cup measure

spatula

1-Tablespoon measure

timer

HEALTHY MEAL TIP

Serve **Turkey Rice Casserole** with **Golden Glazed Carrots** and fresh fruit.

What I Do

1. Wash my hands.

    Place strainer in sink.

2. Measure mushrooms (or peas). Place in strainer. Rinse under cold running water. Set aside.

3. Place skillet on stove. Unwrap turkey. Put in skillet.

4. Throw away meat wrapper. Wash my hands. Clean counter (see page 11).

5. Cook turkey in skillet until all meat is brown. Turn heat to LOW.

6. Open soup with can opener. Use spatula to scrape soup into skillet.

7. Add to skillet and mix well—
   - mushrooms (or peas)
   - onion soup mix
   - cooked rice

8. Put lid on skillet.

 Wash my hands.

9.  Set timer for 15 minutes. When timer goes off, turn off stove.

Serve and ENJOY!

Chili

Number of Servings

This recipe makes 6 servings
1 serving = 1 cup

Meal Planning

Protein and vegetables

What I Need

1	pound extra lean ground beef
1	cup frozen or fresh chopped onion
2	(15-ounce) cans kidney beans
1	(10.75-ounce) can no-added-salt tomato soup
1	Tablespoon plus 1 teaspoon chili powder

Dash of black pepper

What I Use

large deep skillet with lid

can opener

1-cup measure

wooden spoon

spatula

1-Tablespoon measure

1-teaspoon measure

timer

cutting board (for fresh onion)

sharp knife (for fresh onion)

HEALTHY MEAL TIP

Serve **Chili** with fresh **Lettuce & Tomato Salad**, whole grain crackers, and **Yogurt & Fruit Parfait**.

What I Do

1. Wash my hands.

2. Unwrap beef; put in skillet. Throw away meat wrapper.

    Wash my hands. Clean counter (see page 11).

3. If using fresh onion: On cutting board, chop it into tiny pieces with sharp knife. Measure onion and pour into skillet. Place skillet on stove.

4. Cook meat and onions on MEDIUM heat. Stir with wooden spoon. Cook until all meat is brown.

5. Open 2 cans of beans with can opener. Do not drain. Use spatula to scrape all beans into skillet.

6. Open soup with can opener. Use spatula to scrape soup into skillet.

7. Add to skillet and mix well—
   - chili powder
   - pepper

8. Cover skillet with lid. Turn heat to LOW.

    Wash my hands.

    Set timer for 1 hour. Stir now and then.

9. When timer goes off, turn off stove.

Serve and ENJOY!

Chili Macaroni

Number of Servings

This recipe makes 6 servings
1 serving = 1 cup

Meal Planning

Protein and grains

What I Need

4   cups water

2   cups whole grain elbow macaroni (dry)

1   (15-ounce) can chili with beans

1   (8-ounce) can no-added-salt tomato sauce

½   teaspoon chili powder

What I Use

large pot

large deep skillet

strainer

can opener

1-cup measure

wooden spoon and spatula

½-teaspoon measure

timer

HEALTHY MEAL TIP

Serve **Chili Macaroni** with **Speedy Tossed Salad** and **Baked Apple**.

What I Do

1. Wash my hands.

    Place strainer in sink.

2. Measure water and pour into pot. Place pot on stove. Turn stove to HIGH until water boils.

3. Carefully add macaroni to boiling water.

4. Lower heat to MEDIUM LOW.

   Set timer for 10 minutes. Stir every 2 to 3 minutes.

5. Open chili with can opener. Use spatula to scrape chili into skillet.

6. Open tomato sauce with can opener. Use spatula to scrape sauce into skillet. Stir well.

7. Measure and add chili powder.

8. Heat chili and sauce in skillet on MEDIUM until bubbly.

9. When timer goes off, turn off stove under macaroni. Carefully pour macaroni and water into strainer in sink. Ask for help if the pot is too heavy.

10. Pour drained macaroni into skillet with chili.

11. Stir well. Turn off stove.

 Wash my hands.

Serve and ENJOY!

Chinese Pork

Number of Servings

This recipe makes 4 servings
1 serving = 1 cup pork over ½ cup rice

Meal Planning

Protein, vegetables, and grains

What I Need

1   recipe Instant Brown Rice, prepared (page 20)
2   celery ribs (1 cup chopped)
1   pound boneless, lean pork loin
1   Tablespoon olive oil
½   cup frozen or fresh chopped onion
1   (10.75-ounce) can reduced-sodium, low-fat cream of mushroom soup
1   (12-ounce) bag frozen stir-fry vegetables
2   Tablespoons low-sodium soy sauce
1   teaspoon ground ginger

What I Use

4 serving plates
large deep skillet with lid
small bowl
can opener
scissors

cutting board
sharp knife
½-cup measure
wooden spoon
measuring spoons
timer

HEALTHY MEAL TIP

Serve **Chinese Pork** with **Apple Grape Salad**. Enjoy a small glass of cold low-fat milk.

What I Do

1. Wash my hands.

2. Rinse celery under cold running water. Remove all dirt.

3. On cutting board, use sharp knife to cut celery and onion (if using fresh) in small pieces. Add celery and onion to small bowl.

4. Unwrap pork. Place pork on cutting board. Throw away meat wrapper.
 Wash my hands.

5. On cutting board, cut pork in small pieces with sharp knife.
 Wash my hands. Clean counter (see page 11).

6. Measure oil. Add to skillet. Place skillet on stove. Turn stove to MEDIUM heat.

7. Add pork to skillet. Cook pork until white. Stir as it cooks.

8. With wooden spoon, push pork to side of skillet. Add onion and celery to skillet. Cook till vegetables are soft (about 5 minutes).

9. Open soup can. Use spoon to scrape soup into skillet.

10. Add to skillet and stir well—
   • soy sauce
   • ginger
   • stir-fry vegetables

11. Cover skillet. Turn to LOW heat.
 Wash my hands.
 Set timer for 15 minutes.

12. When timer goes off, turn off stove.

13. Measure ½ cup cooked rice on each plate and cover with Chinese pork.

Serve and ENJOY!

Meat Loaf

Number of Servings

This recipe makes 5 servings
1 serving = 1 slice

Meal Planning

Protein and grains

What I Need

Nonstick cooking spray

1	egg
½	cup ketchup
1	pound extra lean ground beef or lean ground turkey
2	slices whole grain bread
1	cup frozen or fresh chopped onion
1	Tablespoon salt-free Italian herb seasoning

What I Use

9 × 5 × 3-inch loaf pan

large mixing bowl

1-cup measure

½-cup measure

fork and turner

1-Tablespoon measure

timer

oven mitt and pot holder

cutting board and sharp knife (for fresh onion)

food thermometer

HEALTHY MEAL TIP

Serve **Meat Loaf** with **Baked Potato** and **Microwave Frozen Vegetables**.

What I Do

1. Wash my hands.

    Preheat oven to 350°F. Spray loaf pan with cooking spray.

2. Break egg into bowl. Throw away shells.

    Wash my hands.

3. Mix egg with fork until bubbly.

4. Measure and add ketchup to bowl. Use fork to mix well.

5. Unwrap meat. Place in bowl. Throw away wrapper.

    Wash my hands. Clean counter (see page 11).

6. Break 2 bread slices into small pieces.

7. If using fresh onion: On cutting board, chop onion into small pieces with sharp knife.

8. Measure and add to bowl—
   • bread pieces   • onion
   • Italian seasoning

9. Use hands or fork to mix well. Place meat into loaf pan. Pat top lightly.

    Wash my hands.

10. Put loaf pan in oven.

     Set timer for 50 minutes.

11. When timer goes off, carefully remove loaf pan from oven with oven mitt and pot holder. Use food thermometer (see pages 12, 16). Turn off oven.

12. Let sit for 5 minutes.

13. Use turner to cut meat loaf into 5 slices. Remove slices from loaf pan with turner.

Serve and ENJOY!

Meatballs

Number of Servings

This recipe makes 6 servings
1 serving = 3 meatballs

Meal Planning

Protein and grains

What I Need

1   pound extra lean ground beef
1   small onion
1   slice whole grain bread
1   egg
2   Tablespoons skim milk
2   Tablespoons Worcestershire sauce
Dash of black pepper
1½ cups spaghetti sauce

What I Use

serving plates

9-inch glass pie plate

medium mixing bowl

small mixing bowl

cutting board and sharp knife

¼-cup measure

fork

1-Tablespoon measure

wax paper

oven mitt and pot holder

food thermometer

HEALTHY MEAL TIP

Serve **Meatballs** with **Spaghetti for Four**, **Pineapple Cabbage Salad**, and garlic toast.

What I Do

1. Wash my hands.

2. Unwrap beef. Put in medium bowl. Throw meat wrapper in trash.

    Wash my hands. Clean counter (see page 11).

3. Use fork to break meat into small pieces.

4. On cutting board, chop onion in small pieces with sharp knife. Add to meat. Mix well with fork.

5. Crumble bread in small pieces. Add crumbs to meat.

6. Break egg into small bowl. Beat egg with fork until egg is bubbly.

7. Measure and stir into bowl with egg—
   - milk
   - pepper
   - Worcestershire sauce

8. Add egg-milk mixture to meat. Mix well.

9. With hands, shape 18 round meatballs. Place meatballs on pie plate.

    Wash my hands.

10. Cover meatballs with wax paper. Put in microwave. Microwave on HIGH POWER for 5 to 7 minutes.

11. Use oven mitt and pot holder to remove from microwave. Use food thermometer. (See pages 12, 16.)

12. Remove meatballs from pie plate. Place on plates with spaghetti sauce.

Serve and ENJOY!

Pork Chop Apple Bake

Number of Servings

This recipe makes 3 servings
1 serving = 1 pork chop

Meal Planning

Protein and fruits

What I Need

Nonstick cooking spray

1 Tablespoon olive oil

3 lean boneless pork chops
  (4 ounces each)

½ cup frozen or fresh chopped onion

¼ cup whole grain croutons

½ teaspoon parsley flakes

Dash of black pepper

2 medium apples

What I Use

large skillet

7 × 11-inch baking dish

½-cup, ¼-cup, and
½-teaspoon measures

cutting board and sharp knife

fork

aluminum foil

timer

oven mitts

HEALTHY MEAL TIP

Serve **Pork Chop Apple Bake**
with **Microwave Vegetables** and
Florida Citrus Salad.

What I Do

1. Wash my hands.

 Preheat oven to 375°F. Spray baking dish with cooking spray.

2. Measure oil. Pour into skillet.

3. Unwrap chops. Place chops in skillet. Throw away wrapper.

 Wash my hands.
Clean counter (see page 11).

4. Place skillet on stove. Turn stove to MEDIUM heat. Brown chops on both sides. Turn with fork.

5. Use fork to move chops to baking dish. Turn off stove.

6. If using fresh onion: On cutting board, chop onion into small pieces with sharp knife.

7. Measure and sprinkle on chops—
- onions
- parsley
- croutons
- pepper

8. On cutting board, use sharp knife to cut each apple in half and half again. Remove core and throw away. Cut apple into slices. Lay slices on top of chops.

9. Cover baking dish with aluminum foil.

 Wash my hands.

10. Set timer for 40 minutes. Put baking dish in oven. When timer goes off, remove dish with oven mitts and turn off oven.

Serve and ENJOY!

Smothered Pork Chops

Number of Servings

This recipe makes 4 servings
1 serving = 1 pork chop and ½ cup rice

Meal Planning

Protein and grains

What I Need

Nonstick cooking spray

1   Tablespoon olive oil

4   lean boneless pork chops
    (4 ounces each)

¾   cup brown rice (dry, not instant)

½   cup frozen or fresh chopped onion

Dash of black pepper

1   lemon

1   (10.75-ounce) can reduced-
    sodium, low-fat cream of
    mushroom soup

1¾ cups water

What I Use

large skillet

9 × 9-inch baking
dish

medium mixing
bowl

can opener

cutting board and
sharp knife

1-cup, ¾-cup, and
½-cup measures

fork and spatula

measuring spoons

aluminum foil

timer

oven mitt and pot
holder

food thermometer

HEALTHY MEAL TIP

Serve **Smothered Pork Chop**
with **Stir-Fry Zucchini** and
fresh fruit.

What I Do

1. Wash my hands.

 Preheat oven to 325°F. Spray baking dish with cooking spray.

2. Place skillet on stove. Turn stove to MEDIUM heat.

3. Measure oil. Add to skillet.

4. Unwrap chops. Place chops in skillet. Throw away wrapper.

 Wash my hands. Clean counter (see page 11).

5. Brown chops well on both sides.

6. Measure rice. Spread rice evenly in baking dish.

7. Use fork to place chops on top of rice in baking dish. Turn off stove.

8. If using fresh onion: On cutting board, chop onion into small pieces with sharp knife.

9. Measure onion. Add to top of chops. Sprinkle with pepper.

10. On cutting board, cut lemon into slices with sharp knife. Lay slices on chops.

11. Open soup with can opener. Use spatula to scrape soup into bowl.

12. Measure water. Pour water in bowl. Mix well. Pour soup mixture over chops.

13. Cover dish with aluminum foil. Place in oven. Set timer for 1 hour.

Wash my hands.

14. When timer goes off, remove dish from oven with oven mitts and turn off oven. Use food thermometer. (See pages 12, 16.)

Serve and ENJOY!

Tater Tot Casserole

Number of Servings

This recipe makes 6 servings
1 serving = 1 cup

Meal Planning

Protein and starchy vegetables

What I Need

Nonstick cooking spray

1   pound extra lean ground beef

½   cup frozen or fresh chopped onion

1   (12-ounce) bag frozen mixed vegetables

1   (16-ounce) package frozen Tater Tots (about 50 potato puffs)

1   (10.75-ounce) can reduced-sodium, low-fat cream of mushroom soup

¾   cup skim milk

Dash of black pepper

HEALTHY MEAL TIP

Serve **Tater Tot Casserole** with **Lettuce & Tomato Salad** and fresh fruit.

What I Use

9 × 9-inch baking dish	spatula and wooden spoon
large skillet	timer
medium mixing bowl	oven mitt and pot holder
can opener and scissors	cutting board and sharp knife (fresh onion)
1-cup, ½-cup, and ¾-cup measures	

What I Do

1. Wash my hands.

    Preheat oven to 350°F. Spray baking dish with cooking spray.

2. Unwrap beef and place in skillet. Throw away meat wrapper.

    Wash my hands. Clean counter (see page 11).

3. Place skillet on stove. Use wooden spoon to break up meat.

4. If using fresh onion: On cutting board, chop onion into small pieces with sharp knife.

5. Measure onion. Add to skillet. Turn stove to MEDIUM heat. Mix in onion with wooden spoon.

6. Stir to cook until all meat is brown.

7. Turn off stove. Spoon cooked meat and onion into baking dish.

8. Pour mixed vegetables over meat and onions.

9. Add about 50 potato puffs. Spread around evenly over meat.

 Wash my hands.

10. Open soup with can opener. Use spatula to scrape all soup into bowl.

11. Measure milk. Add milk to soup in bowl. Mix with spatula.

12. Pour soup-milk mixture evenly over casserole. Put baking dish in oven.

 Set timer for 35 minutes.

13. When timer goes off, use oven mitt and pot holder to carefully remove baking dish from oven. Turn off oven.

Serve and ENJOY!

Western Skillet

Number of Servings

This recipe makes 5 servings
1 serving = 1 cup

Meal Planning

Protein and grains

What I Need

1   pound extra lean ground beef

¾   cup instant brown rice (dry)

2   Tablespoons dry onion soup mix

1   (15-ounce) can no-added-salt
     stewed tomatoes

2   cups water

1   cup shredded cheddar cheese

What I Use

large deep skillet with lid

can opener

1-cup measure

¾-cup measure

wooden spoon

1-Tablespoon measure

timer

HEALTHY MEAL TIP

Serve **Western Skillet** with a fresh
garden salad. Add your favorite
pudding.

What I Do

1. Wash my hands.

2. Unwrap beef. Place in large skillet. Throw away meat wrapper.

    Wash my hands. Clean counter (see page 11).

3. Place skillet on stove. Set stove to MEDIUM heat.

4. Break up beef with wooden spoon. Stir. Cook until all meat is brown.

5. Set stove to LOW heat.

6. Measure and add to skillet—
   - brown rice
   - tomatoes
   - onion soup mix
   - 2 cups water

7. Stir well. Cover with lid. Keep stove at LOW heat.

    Wash my hands.

8. Set timer for 25 minutes and cook.

9. When timer goes off, add cheese to top of meat mixture.

10. Cover and set timer for 5 minutes.

11. When timer goes off, turn off stove. Cheese should be nearly melted.

Serve and ENJOY!

Healthy Restaurant Choices

Eating out is fun. Eating out can also be healthy. Almost every restaurant (quick service or sit down) has at least one healthy (or healthier) menu choice. Talk to the wait staff (your waitress or waiter). Ask them how the food is made.

Here are 13 things I can do to choose healthy foods when eating out:

1. Order a small hamburger (one patty; not two) with lots of fresh vegetables like lettuce, tomato, and onion.

2. Order foods that are roasted or grilled (like roasted chicken or grilled fish).

3. Order foods that are baked or broiled in place of fried or breaded (like a baked potato in place of french fries).

4. Hold the mayo. Ask if light mayo is used or use mustard, ketchup, or salsa.

5. Hold the cheese. Enjoy cheese at home when I can choose low-fat cheese or string cheese.

6. Order vegetables—fresh, steamed, or baked.

7. Order a garden salad with the dressing "on the side." Then, use only half of the dressing.

8. Split a large meal with a friend.

9. Drink water. Water has no calories and refills are free.

10. Ask for fruit as a side dish in place of hash browns or fried potatoes.

11. Fruit makes a good dessert. If ordering a rich or large dessert, share it with a friend.

12. Ask for a "take-home box" when I place my order. If my meal is large, put some in the box before I start to eat.

13. Order from the "senior" or "kids" menu. These meals are the right amount of food to eat.

Asian

- Asian vegetables like snow peas, bamboo shoots, water chestnuts, cabbage, baby corn, carrots, and broccoli are healthy foods.

- If my meal is large, I'll ask for a "take-home box" and save some to eat later.

- Order any stir-fried vegetable dish with tofu, shrimp, chicken, lean beef, or lean pork.

- Order steamed rice in place of fried rice.

- Order steamed noodles in place of fried noodles.

- Order steamed meat dishes in place of fried, sweet-and-sour, or breaded meat dishes.

Mexican

- Order a burrito, taco, or tostada. Ask for beans, chicken, or combo beans/beef. Ask for less cheese.

- Use extra salsa instead of sour cream.

- Order a beef or chicken taco salad without the shell. Order salsa as a fat-free dressing.

- Mexican rice, black beans, and pinto beans are healthy menu choices.

Pizza

- Pizza is a good food. Eat 2 slices and take the rest home. Leftover pizza is good to eat for another meal.

- Pizza crust—Order thin or hand-tossed. Stay away from deep-dish, thick-crust, or stuffed-crust.

- Pizza toppings—Ask for extra vegetable toppings and tomato sauce. Choose lean meats like Canadian bacon, ham, or chicken. Order a cheese pizza.

Healthy Dining Finder

Get help making smart menu choices. Visit *healthydiningfinder.com* to look for healthy menu items at my favorite or any restaurant.

Healthy Snacks

Snacks to Eat at Home and Work

Plan a healthy snack before I leave home. A snack can be healthy and help me not overeat at the next meal. I will choose healthy snacks that give me energy without a lot of calories, fat, sugar, or salt.

Here are good snack choices from each food group:

GRAINS 	graham crackers (2) granola bar, low calorie (1) popcorn, air-popped or microwave (3 cups) pretzels (1 ounce or 12 large twist-style) whole wheat crackers (6)
VEGETABLES 	any fresh vegetable (1 piece) baby carrots (12) bag of fresh vegetable slices (cucumber, broccoli, cauliflower, celery; 8 pieces) can of low-sodium tomato juice or vegetable juice (6 ounces) leftover microwave vegetables (½ cup)
FRUITS 	applesauce, 1 (4 ounce) prepackaged snack fresh fruit (1 piece) fruit cup, 1 (4 ounce) prepackaged snack gelatin cup with fruit, 1 (4 ounce) prepackaged snack mixed dried fruit (raisins, cranberries; 1 mini box or 2 tablespoons)
DAIRY 	hot cocoa, low-calorie (1 packet) low-fat cheese (1 ounce) milk, low-fat or skim (½ cup or 1 carton) string cheese (1 prepackaged snack) yogurt, low-fat (6 ounces)
PROTEIN 	hard-cooked egg (1) nuts (6 to 8) peanut butter (1 Tablespoon) on a slice of whole grain bread or whole wheat crackers (6) trail mix (pretzels, nuts, raisins, cereals, dried fruit; 1 to 2 ounces) tuna (¼ cup) on a slice of whole grain bread

Don't forget that leftovers from any of the recipes in *Let's Cook!* can make a good snack. Leftovers don't cost extra money. Keep leftover food cold until I can eat it.

Snacks from the Vending Machine

Snack machines are often filled with foods that are high in calories, fat, sugar, or salt. Choose wisely.

I will look for these fun and healthy snacks:

GRAINS 	granola bar or fig bar mini box of cereal small bag of microwave popcorn small bag of pretzels or animal crackers
VEGETABLES	bag of fresh mixed vegetables or baby carrots can of tomato juice or vegetable juice garden salad with fat-free dressing soup
FRUITS 	fresh fruit (apple, orange, banana) gelatin with fruit or applesauce small box of raisins or cranberries small can of fruit juice (not fruit drink)
DAIRY 	cheese and crackers (not sandwich-type) low-fat milk/chocolate milk pudding or yogurt string cheese
PROTEIN 	peanut butter and crackers (not sandwich-type) small bag of peanuts, nuts, or sunflower seeds small bag of trail mix small sandwich

What to drink? Bottled water or water from a drinking fountain is always a healthy choice. Water is better than regular soda (pop) or diet soda (pop).

Nutrient Analysis

Recipes

	Serving Size	Calories	Protein (grams)	Carbohydrate (grams)	Carbohydrate Choices	Fat (grams)	Saturated Fat (grams)	Sodium (milligrams)	Fiber (grams)	Diabetic Exchanges
GRAINS (pp. 18–31)										
Indian Rice (p. 18)	¾ cup	150	3	32	2	1	0	55	3	2 starch
Instant Brown Rice (p. 20)	½ cup	110	3	23	1½	1	0	5	1	1½ starch
Rice Vegetable Medley (p. 22)	¾ cup	130	4	24	1½	2	0.5	160	2	1 starch, 1 vegetable
Saucepan Spaghetti (p. 24)	1½ cups	330	26	34	2	12	6	230	6	2 starch, 1 vegetable, 3 lean meat
Spaghetti for Four (p. 26)	½ cup	150	6	21	1½	5	1.5	80	4	1½ starch, 1 fat
Spanish Rice (p. 28)	¾ cup	230	11	32	2	5	1	460	4	2 starch, 1 lean meat, 1 fat
Tortilla Sandwich Wrap (p. 30)	1 wrap	230	19	28	2	3	0	820	3	2 starch, 2 lean meat
NONSTARCHY VEGETABLES (pp. 32–43)										
Golden Glazed Carrots (p. 32)	½ cup	90	1	12	1	5	0.5	30	1	2 vegetable, 1 fat
Lettuce & Tomato Salad (p. 34)	1 salad	40	2	8	½	0	0	270	1	1½ vegetable
Microwave Vegetables (p. 36)	½ cup	60	2	9	½	2	1	115	2	2 vegetable
Speedy Tossed Salad (p. 38)	1 cup	70	2	9	½	4	0	140	3	1½ vegetable, 1 fat
Spinach Apple Salad (p. 40)	1 salad	150	1	27	2	6	0	210	4	1 vegetable, 1½ fruit, 1 fat
Stir-Fry Zucchini (p. 42)	½ cup	0	0	0	0	0	0	0	0	Free!
STARCHY VEGETABLES (pp. 44–57)										
Baked Potato (p. 44)	1 potato	160	5	32	2	3	2	45	2	2 starch
Confetti Corn (p. 46)	½ cup	170	4	17	1	8	2.5	250	2	1 starch, 1 fat
Corn Chowder (p. 48)	1 cup	160	6	32	2	6	2	260	2	1 starch, 1 skim milk
Gingered Sweet Potatoes (p. 50)	1 potato	110	2	25	1½	0	0	55	3	1½ starch
Mashed Potatoes & Carrots (p. 52)	½ cup	80	2	16	1	0	0	390	2	1 starch
Pea Salad (p. 54)	½ cup	130	6	15	1	6	0	210	3	1 starch, 1 fat
Super Spud (p. 56)	1 potato	200	10	40	2	2	1	460	6	1 starch, 1 skim milk
FRUITS (pp. 58–69)										
Apple Grape Salad (p. 58)	¾ cup	170	2	27	2	8	1	45	3	2 fruit, 1 fat
Apple Slaw (p. 60)	¾ cup	80	3	17	1	0	0	40	2	1 fruit, 1 vegetable
Baked Apple (p. 62)	1 apple	130	1	27	2	4	0	30	3	2 fruit
Florida Citrus Salad (p. 64)	¾ cup	60	2	14	1	0	0	20	1	1 fruit
Pineapple Cabbage Salad (p. 66)	1 cup	130	3	33	2	0	0	140	3	1½ fruit, 2 vegetable
Pineapple Carrot Salad (p. 68)	1 salad	130	2	32	2	0	0	45	2	2 fruit, 1 vegetable

Recipes

	Serving Size	Calories	Protein (grams)	Carbohydrate (grams)	Carbohydrate Choices	Fat (grams)	Saturated Fat (grams)	Sodium (milligrams)	Fiber (grams)	Diabetic Exchanges
DAIRY (pp. 70–81)										
Broccoli Cheese Soup (p. 70)	1 cup	340	21	18	1	9	2.5	390	3	2 reduced-fat milk, 1 vegetable
Cottage Cheese Tomato Salad (p. 72)	1 salad	100	15	7	½	2	1	460	1	½ skim milk, 1 veg., 1 lean meat
Easy Cheese Quesadilla (p. 74)	1 quesadilla	430	17	49	3	18	7	770	4	2 reduced-fat milk, 2 starch, 1 fat
Fruit Smoothie (p. 76)	1 smoothie	230	12	42	3	2	1	140	4	1½ skim milk, 1½ fruit
Sunflower Salad (p. 78)	1 salad	180	10	25	2	6	0	430	2	1 skim milk, 1 fruit, ½ fat
Yogurt & Fruit Parfait (p. 80)	1 parfait	200	12	34	2	2	1	160	3	1½ skim milk, 1 fruit
PROTEIN – EGGS (pp. 82–85)										
French Toast & Breakfast Links (p. 82)	2 toast/2 links	330	23	32	2	11	3.5	690	5	2 starch, 3 lean meat
Veggie Omelet (p. 84)	1 omelet	120	11	4	0	6	2	190	1	2 lean meat
PROTEIN – FISH (pp. 86–95)										
Baked Salmon (p. 86)	3 ounces	170	22	2	0	7	1	200	1	3 lean meat
Fish Sandwich (p. 88)	1 sandwich	310	27	26	2	11	4.5	740	3	2 starch, 3 lean meat
Tuna Apple Salad (p. 90)	¾ cup	150	14	12	1	6	0	310	2	1 fruit, 2 lean meat
Tuna Burger (p. 92)	1 burger	240	23	26	2	6	1	590	4	2 starch, 3 lean meat
Tuna Pasta Salad (p. 94)	1 cup	230	15	33	2	6	0	270	3	2 starch, 2 lean meat
PROTEIN – CHICKEN & TURKEY (pp. 96–107)										
Apricot Curry Chicken (p. 96)	3 ounces	190	26	11	1	3	1	100	0	1 fruit, 3 lean meat
Baked Chicken (p. 98)	3 ounces	170	23	3	0	7	1	510	0	3 lean meat
Chicken Stir-Fry (p. 100)	1 cup	230	26	16	1	6	0.5	730	3	3 vegetable, 3 lean meat
Creamed Chicken over Rice (p. 102)	1 cup w/rice	250	20	20	1	10	1.5	75	2	1 starch, 3 lean meat
Turkey Burger (p. 104)	1 burger	220	25	25	2	4	0	500	3	2 starch, 2½ lean meat
Turkey Rice Casserole (p. 106)	1 cup	190	30	13	1	2	0	390	1	1 starch, 3 lean meat
PROTEIN – BEEF & PORK (pp. 108–125)										
Chili (p. 108)	1 cup	230	24	28	1½	3	1	430	7	1½ starch, 3 lean meat
Chili Macaroni (p. 110)	1 cup	190	9	42	2½	1	0	330	7	2½ starch
Chinese Pork (p. 112)	1 cup w/rice	280	21	21	1½	10	3	650	4	1 starch, 1 vegetable, 3 lean meat
Meat Loaf (p. 114)	1 slice	160	18	14	1	4	1.5	370	1	1 starch, 2 lean meat
Meatballs (p. 116)	3 meatballs	170	14	16	1	6	1.5	400	3	1 starch, 2 lean meat
Pork Chop Apple Bake (p. 118)	1 chop	230	19	17	1	10	2.5	65	3	1 fruit, 3 lean meat
Smothered Pork Chops (p. 120)	1 chop w/rice	300	21	35	2	12	3.5	70	2	2 starch, 3 lean meat
Tater Tot Casserole (p. 122)	1 cup	290	20	27	2	12	3	270	4	1 starch, 3 lean meat
Western Skillet (p. 124)	1 cup	230	26	19	1	5	2	460	3	1 starch, 3 lean meat

Index

Conversion Charts

Weighted ingredient	US	Metric
b		
bell pepper, chopped	½ cup	54 g
blueberries, fresh	½ cup	65 g
blueberries, frozen	½ cup	60 g
brown rice, cooked	1 cup	195 g
brown rice, dry	1 cup	180 g
c		
cabbage or slaw, shredded	1 cup	90 g
carrots, baby	1½ cups	200 g
carrots, shredded (prepackaged)	½ cup	34 g
celery, chopped	¼ cup	34 g
cheddar, shredded	1 cup	130 g
cottage cheese	½ cup	112 g
cranberries, dried	¼ cup	30 g
croutons	¼ cup	18 g
l		
lettuce greens (prepackaged)	1½ cups	48 g
m		
macaroni, elbow, dry	1 cup	100 g
mixed vegetables, frozen	1 cup	133 g
mozzarella, shredded	1 cup	110 g
mushrooms, sliced fresh (prepackaged)	½ cup	35 g
o		
onion, fresh, chopped	1 cup	160 g
onion, frozen, chopped	1 cup	210 g
p		
Parmesan, shredded	¼ cup	20 g
peas, frozen	1 cup	134 g
r		
raisins	¼ cup	39 g
s		
spinach, baby	2 cups	43 g
strawberries, fresh	½ cup	85 g
strawberries, frozen	½ cup	68 g
w		
walnuts, chopped	¼ cup	30 g
y		
yogurt, low-fat	½ cup	122 g

Cooking Temperatures for Meat

Chicken, turkey	165°F	74°C
Egg dishes	160°F	71°C
Fish	145°F	63°C
Ground beef, pork	160°F	71°C
Leftovers	165°F	74°C
Roasts and chops	145–160°F	63–71°C

Oven Temperatures

325°F	165°C	3 gas
350°F	180°C	4 gas
375°F	190°C	5 gas
400°F	200°C	6 gas
425°F	220°C	7 gas

Liquids

US	Metric
1 fluid ounce	30 ml
1 cup	240 ml

Weight

US/Imperial	Metric
1 ounce	28 g
1 pound	½ kg

Acknowledgments

When Sarah was a teenager, I encouraged her to develop meal-planning and cooking skills, hoping those skills would enable Sarah to enjoy a healthy lifestyle as an adult.

Sincere appreciation is extended to the following:

Sarah's teachers and community agency staff who assisted Sarah in learning to cook.

Special education teachers in the Iowa City Community School District (Iowa), who developed some of Sarah's recipes and arranged time for cooking in school. In her first years of high school, Sarah's teachers Shannon Sullivan-Channon and Molly Abraham introduced healthy meal-planning and shopping skills.

Staff from Life Skills, Inc., of Iowa City who guided Sarah to prepare lunch and dinner foods twice a week for more than ten years while Sarah lived with her parents.

In Sarah's beginning days of cooking, recipes from two sources inspired us:

The Children's Cookbook: A Beginner's Guide to Cooking (1980). Nashville: Famous Recipes Press.
Step-by-Step Pictorial Cookbook. (1980). St. Louis, MO: Ralston Purina Company.

The source for adaptation of the Spanish Rice recipe was:

Jean Bunnell. *62 Easy and Delicious Cooking Activities*. (1986). Portland, ME: Walch Publishing.

Others who helped include:

Amelia Kurth, sister of William Kurth, Sarah's classmate, who returned to Iowa City from California for two months to develop recipes that would help William control his weight. Some of her recipes were adapted for this book.

Residents and staff at Systems Unlimited, Inc., of Iowa City who tested some of the recipes in residential settings.

—Elizabeth (Betsy) D. Riesz, PhD

I would like to acknowledge two women who influenced both my professional development and my undertaking of this book:

Linda Snetselaar, PhD, RD/LD, who was my professor and graduate advisor at the University of Iowa School of Public Health.

Anne Tabor, MPH, RD/LD, nutrition supervisor, Center for Disabilities and Development, and training director for Iowa's Leadership Education in Neurodevelopmental and Related Disabilities Project at the University of Iowa Hospitals and Clinics. Ms. Tabor was my preceptor during my interdisciplinary leadership training at the Center for Disabilities and Development.

Anne Tabor also provided workshops on healthy foods, menu planning, and exercise for Sarah, her housemates, and staff prior to Sarah's move to supported living. It is Ms. Tabor who first suggested a cookbook be published based on Sarah's recipes.

—Anne Kissack, MPH, RD

This book would not have been possible without the expert guidance and passionate enthusiasm of the Appletree Press project team, headed up by Linda Hachfeld. She believed in this book from the beginning, and her steadfast spirit and compassionate heart engineered the creation of this book.

—Betsy and Anne, coauthors